I Am
the Walrus

I AM THE WALRUS

CONFESSIONS AND TIPS FROM A BLUE-COLLAR GOLFER

BY CRAIG STADLER

WITH JOHN ANDRISANI

Delacorte Press

Published by
Delacorte Press
Bantam Doubleday Dell Publishing Group, Inc.
1540 Broadway
New York, New York 10036

Library of Congress Cataloging in Publication Data
Stadler, Craig.
    I am the Walrus : confessions and tips from a blue-
collar golfer / by Craig Stadler with John Andrisani.
        p.   cm.
    ISBN 0-385-31259-8
    1. Golf.   2. Stadler, Craig.   3. Golfers—United States—
Biography.   I. Andrisani, John.   II. Title.
GV963.S67   1995
796.352—dc20   94-21864
                                                    CIP

Illustrations by Ken Lewis

Photographs by Jeff Blanton

Book design by Susan Maksuta
Manufactured in the United States of America
Published simultaneously in Canada

June 1995

10   9   8   7   6   5   4   3   2   1

BVG

CONTENTS

Foreword by John Andrisani   vii

Introduction   xi

Chapter One   1
THE GREATEST GAME OF ALL:
Highlights and Low Points of My Marriage
with Golf

Chapter Two   23
PRACTICE, PRACTICE, PRACTICE:
How to Have Fun While Mastering Golf's
Scoring Shots

Chapter Three   55
YOU ASKED FOR IT:
Questions Every Golfer Wants the
Answers To

Chapter Four   109
THE RULES RULE:
It Pays to Play by the Book

Chapter Five   145
SUPERTIPS:
Quick Tips on Shotmaking Techniques
for the Golfer on the Run

Biographies   176

FOREWORD

I first met Craig Stadler in 1984. At the time I was on assignment for *Golf Magazine,* where I'd been the instruction editor for two years. My assignment was to interview Stadler for a cover story called "Taming the Rough." The interview took place at the Tournament Players' Club, the PGA Tour's home course in Ponte Vedra, Florida. Our readers, like most of the other millions of golfers in the United States, often hit the ball into the "hay." So naturally, an article by Stadler on how to hit short and long recovery shots onto the green would help our subscribers shave vital strokes off their scores, plus sell well on the newsstands.

Stadler had been on a hot streak since 1980. In 1982, for example, he'd won four tournaments on the PGA Tour, including the prestigious Masters, and finished first on the money list with $446,462.

The first thing I noticed about Stadler—probably the first thing anyone notices—was the girth of his waist and the broadness of his shoulders. He is not all that tall, but he sure is big. His dress code and general demeanor are also striking, particularly given the milieu of professional golf: shirt half in, half out; collar buttons open; loose-fitting baggy pants that kept falling down and he kept pulling up; scuffed shoes; long hair; droopy mustache. Stadler looked more like a blue-collar public golfer than a Tour professional. However, he spoke very articulately and with authority, and got right to the point. There is not a single phony streak in him either. He was then, and remains today, a regular guy with a great sense of humor. I knew right away why "The Walrus" was one of golf's most popular pros.

With a club in his hand Stadler was even more impressive. From the time he lofted his first wedge shot high over a bunker and landed the ball softly onto the green next to the hole, I was convinced, once and for all, that all that stuff I had heard about big guys having no touch was a bunch of bull.

Naturally, the way Stadler ripped a medium iron out of the rough impressed me too. But, owing to his great strength, that was to be expected. What I didn't expect was Stadler's talent as a teacher.

One of the shots Stadler was asked to teach readers was the soft-landing chip, hit out of a snug lie on a steep grassy uphill slope, to a pin about twenty feet away, on a very fast green. Not an easy shot to hit close to the cup.

To help me better understand the instructional message, Stadler had me stand on the slope with a club in my hand, while he explained the proper setup and swing.

"Take a narrow stance; play the ball back slightly; lean most of your weight left, into the slope; set your hands ahead of the ball; close the clubface a little to compensate for its opening at impact," he said, and then added:

Foreword

"You'll want to swing the club back in one piece to knee height, while keeping your wrists firm and weight on your left foot. Coming down, you'll want to pull the club down with both hands."

When it came time to give it a go, I was nervous. I was still considered quite new on the job. The last thing I wanted to get back to the office in New York was that Andrisani choked during the Stadler shoot, fluffing a short shot around the green.

A voice inside my head told me I'd feel safer and would hit a decent shot if I forgot what Stadler said and did things my way. But I couldn't do that. For the sake of job politics and the readers of *Golf,* I had to put my trust in the instruction being given to me by a soft-spoken man who looked more like Popeye's nemesis, Brutus, than the image I held of a golf master.

I swung. The wedge's leading edge cut into the thick grass behind the ball, lofting it straight into the air. The ball landed softly onto the green and then rolled toward the flag, as Stadler said it would. Then it dropped into the hole.

The rest of the session was a breeze, with Stadler simply continuing to communicate different recovery techniques. However, I was never asked to hit another shot. I like to think that was because Stadler thought that I was as good a student as he was a teacher. The important thing was that the cover story was a success. In fact, maybe that's another reason why I was asked to collaborate with him in the writing of *I AM THE WALRUS: Confessions and Tips from a Blue-collar*

Foreword

Golfer. Whatever the reason, I'm happy that I was chosen. Stadler is a wonderful man to spend time with and to learn from.

In this book Stadler tells his fans everything they ever wanted to know about him and about the pro game, including the truth behind the infamous "towel incident." He also covers the basics of practicing and shotmaking, and then the more sophisticated stuff, like what jokes not to tell your boss if you're lucky enough to be invited to his snobbish white-collar private club, and how to throw a club correctly when you want to let off steam on the course. There are even superquick tips for the blue-collar golfer on the run.

I hope you enjoy reading *I AM THE WALRUS* as much as I enjoyed writing it with Craig. I will make one guarantee: if this book doesn't help you lower your handicap, it will lower your blood pressure. Either way, you're a winner!

John Andrisani

INTRODUCTION

A couple of years ago, I got to thinking: Craig, you've given quite a bit back to golf, a game that's been good to you and your family. You've done work for charity, supported the San Diego Junior Golf Association, campaigned for fast play, given clinics to chief executive officers and lessons to your wealthy amateur partners in big pro-am events. But what have you done for the almost twenty million blue-collar public players—the working men and women who wait on line before dawn to get a starting ticket; carry a vinyl bag filled with tube club dividers, store-bought woods, and irons with red plastic covers over their heads; fish the waters with a special scooper and search the woods for other people's lost balls; use a pull cart; and wear inexpensive shirts, pants, and shoes—the people who make up over three-fourths of the total American golf population? My answer was: Nothing.

I decided then that I wanted to write an offbeat book designed to help the blue-collar golfer play a better, more enjoyable game of golf.

My manager, Lynn Roach, contacted John Andrisani, a senior editor of *Golf Magazine*, because he had a great track record of collaborating with top Tour pros on instruction books. Furthermore, he had also written biographical profiles and some humorous short stories. Since the book was to be part biographical and part technical with a

Introduction

tongue-in-cheek twist, that was the combination Roach and I were looking for in a cowriter. The book's title was, of course, *I AM THE WALRUS: Confessions and Tips from a Blue-collar Golfer.*

Two years later—after numerous face-to-face interviews and telephone conversations with Andrisani, and several cassette tapes mailed to him from me—I'm proud of the finished text: one that's enhanced with drawings by British-based artist Ken Lewis and photographs by Jeff Blanton.

If you're not already a fan of mine, I hope you'll be one after reading *I AM THE WALRUS.* This book is truly an intimate account of my personal and professional life. However, there's more: How to hit the tough shots you only run into on those rugged, less-manicured public courses; how to prepare for a round with your boss; how to practice with a beer in your hand; how to play by the rules so you don't embarrass yourself; what drink to order at the nineteenth hole; and what restaurants to hang out in if you happen to be following the Tour.

Before moving on to the first chapter, I'd like to present my dedication of this book. Usually, of course, an author will credit his parents, his wife, or someone else near and dear to him or her for inspiring and guiding the book-writing undertaking. I'm going to break the mold here, because throughout the book I talk about how important my wife, my family, and my teachers have been in furthering my career. They won't be upset if I don't dedicate it to them. So, as the resident blue-

Introduction

collar representative of the PGA Tour, I hereby
dedicate this book to the Los Angeles Kings
hockey team. I'm a monster fan of the Wayne
Gretzky–led Kings and of hockey in general. What
better dedication by a blue-collar athlete than
that?

Reading this book will teach you to forget your
problems and Play Golf for Enjoyment. Not one
true blue-collar golfer who has ever played hooky
from work to visit the links has ever forgotten
that motto. Let it be yours forever.

Craig Stadler

I Am
the Walrus

1
The Greatest Game of All:

Highlights and Low Points of My Marriage with Golf

I think we would all agree that the walrus is a pretty unassuming sea animal—a true character that just shuffles along the shoreline in the Arctic, casually snatching a fish whenever appetite dictates, or sleeping whenever the urge comes. The walrus gets along just fine without causing a stir.

Frankly, I'm pretty laid back too. (Unless of course I miss a two-foot putt or hit a drive deep into the woods!) But the real reason the fans call me "The Walrus" has little to do with my no-nonsense, easygoing personality. Rather, like the walrus, I sport a heavy mustache with drooping ends, look lazy, and am characterized by a heavy layer of blubber.

At any rate, as one who has accepted this moniker good-naturedly, and as a person who has never actively sought the spotlight, I look back in wonderment at my career and my high standing in the sport of professional golf.

Over the years I've gradually built up a following that stands out at most PGA Tour events. I don't attract many of the upper-crust fans, those who like to follow the players with the most graceful and elegant swings. Come to think of it, that makes perfect sense, because my swing could never be classified as either graceful or elegant. No, my fans at Tour events are mainly the swashbucklers, the blue-collar, public links kind of guys—the golf equivalent of the Oakland Raiders football fans. They're not out to give anyone a hard time, of course. They just want to root for somebody who looks like an everyday Joe instead of someone who looks like he just stepped out of *Esquire*. In that regard, I guess I fit the bill.

Another reason I'm popular with blue-collar golfers is that in the past, I've been known to vent my frustration on the course—just like they do. For example, I long ago mastered the art, after an indifferent iron shot, of tossing the club high into the air, or throwing it down rather forcefully so that its head knifes into the ground and its shaft stands upright, quivering like a tuning fork. I guess they relate to that. I'll teach you how to perfect the true blue-collar Fun Fling technique at the end of Chapter Five.

There's a percentage of golf fans who'll always root for the guy with the girth, the guy whose swing is often less than classical, and whose temperament is closer to Jack Nicholson's (who not so long ago battered a guy's Mercedes with a golf club) than Jack Nicklaus's. So the more I think about it, the more I understand the growth in popularity I've enjoyed over the years that allows me to announce to the world, "I am the Walrus."

Of course, in addition to the personality side of it, to build up a loyal following I've had to play some pretty good golf along the way. And believe me, I've surprised myself. If you'd told me twenty-five years ago all the accomplishments I'd achieve in my career, frankly, I'd have laughed in your face. Yet, and I don't mean to brag, look what's happened in the last two decades or so:

- Won the 1973 NCAA individual championship.
- Won sixteen professional championships (eleven official PGA Tour events and two unofficial ones, along with three foreign titles).
- Won the Masters in 1982.
- Was the PGA Tour's leading money winner in 1982 and finished second on the money list in 1991.
- Have earned over $5.5 million in official PGA Tour earnings alone.

Even though at times I've become frustrated with my performances, whenever I go back and look at the big picture, what has transpired truly amazes me.

EARLY DEVELOPMENT OF THE WALRUS

There was never a grand plan for me to be a PGA Tour player. I really wasn't one of these prodigies who was pushed, prodded, and cajoled to make a concerted lifelong effort to reach a lofty goal. From the outset, I just loved to play golf. And, basically, I've just followed the game wherever it's led me.

I do feel very fortunate that I was introduced to the game at around age five by my dad, Don. There's no substitute for having a cut-down club in your hands from the time you are first able to swing one. To me golf is a game of feel, of repetition after repetition, of the development of a sort of physical intuition by which you learn to hit the golf ball square and true. It's a tremendous advantage to have started the learning process at an early age.

Contrary to what you might think, given my blue-collar image, I can't honestly brag about a deprived early home life followed by a rags-to-riches ascent to the Tour. We were a pretty comfortable, but not wealthy, family. My father was a pharmacist in San Diego, California, where I grew up. He didn't get to play an awful lot of golf. Usually he got out on Wednesdays with many of the doctors he did business with. Dad was a respectable player, but he didn't pretend to be so expert that he should be my personal coach. He didn't pressure me to play. Instead he supported me as my own interest toward golf evolved more and more.

By the time I was seven or eight years of age I had begun entering local peewee golf events. So I had a really full junior career—about ten years, actually. At age eight I got my first, though informal, golf lessons at a course called Presidio Hills, in the old section of San Diego. My teacher was a real old-timer named Al Abrego. I'm guessing he was close to eighty back then, but since I was only eight myself,

I AM THE WALRUS

I could have been pretty far off. Anyway, Mr. Abrego mostly just sat on a stool, feeding me balls one at a time and watching me swing. He must have liked my swing, because he didn't insist on a lot of changes. In fact, he didn't say much at all.

The practice range at Presidio Hills was only about eighty yards long. In my second year there, at age nine, I started hitting my eight-iron over the fence and into the street beyond. That's when Mr. Abrego said that about wrapped it up, there wasn't anything else he felt he could teach me. I still wonder if he really liked my swing, or if he thought he'd better cut me off before I cost him a lot of golf balls.

At about this same time, I benefitted tremendously from the fact that my dad was able to become a member at La Jolla Country Club. That became the home base for most of my junior golf development, and it was a wonderful place to learn the game. La Jolla had character, variety, and balance. Several holes were fairly short but tight, others were long but more open, and the fairways were very undulating. Therefore, playing La Jolla helped me develop a wide array of shots while I was still quite young. I rarely came upon any other courses in later years that demanded things I hadn't encountered at La Jolla.

I really began to get serious about golf at age twelve. That's when I basically gave up baseball and other team sports. I liked the individual challenges that golf alone presented. Also, I'd pretty well determined I'd never be a fleet center fielder or a threat to steal a lot of bases by then. I couldn't dunk a basketball either.

Craig Stadler

From about 1965 on, I'd say my life was pretty well centered around the golf course. When grade school was in session, I'd hit balls every afternoon into the three hundred yards or so of open land that abutted the backyard of our house. During my adolescent years I made my spending money caddying on weekends at nearby Wilshire Country Club—usually carrying doubles in the mornings and getting out on La Jolla in the afternoons.

For those of you who are big on record keeping, I have to confess that I tended to take milestones in stride. That's why I can't remember the first time or place I broke par. But I know I reached "red figures" from the men's tees by the time I was fourteen.

I didn't really have a teacher after Mr. Abrego until about age thirteen, when I took lessons from John Hulbert, who was an assistant pro under Paul Runyan, the former PGA champion. Runyan himself was a renowned teacher, but at that time I was a little too young and dumb to understand Paul's very intricate, technical teaching methods. But working with John Hulbert for a total of four years gave my game a big boost.

In continuing my early golf study program, I'd watch the pros play whenever they competed in tournaments—in Palm Springs, San Diego, or Los Angeles. I never copied any single player's swing, but if I did have an idol, it was definitely Arnold Palmer. Even then I could recognize Arnie's flat-out, go-for-it attitude, and I think mimicking that approach has helped me greatly. If I'm on my game, I have that killer instinct and I almost never lay up.

I AM THE WALRUS

HEADING TOWARD THE BIG TIME

By the time I finished high school, I was a pretty good amateur player. I had just won the 1971 World Junior Championship and had earned a golf scholarship to the University of Southern California. College was terrific, the best time of my life. I guess it was during this stage that I got into some enthusiastic beer drinking, developed a gut, let my hair get out of control, and generally took on my semiunkempt blue-collar image. I didn't study much, either, although I'm proud to say I eventually earned my degree.

But, mostly, my college years were about competing at golf. Again, I don't want to sound immodest, but I was usually the player to beat. During my four years at Southern Cal I won eleven collegiate events, plus a stash of other amateur titles. However, my college golf was not quite as competitive in the early seventies as it might be now. At that time Southern Cal was in the Pac-8 Conference. It hadn't yet expanded to become the Pac-10 and include Arizona and Arizona State, two big-time programs. Other than playing in the annual NCAAs, where we'd meet teams like Florida, Texas, and Wake Forest, the fields I played against weren't the best in college golf. Nevertheless, I did develop a lot as a player.

Another positive influence on my game came in the person of Stan Wood, USC's head coach. Stan didn't try to change much about my long game, but he really took me under his wing regarding the putting game. It was during the USC years that this part of my game really started to blossom. Stan helped me move from being a good putter to, well, a great one. I've told you I don't like to brag; but, heck, it's true. During my first five or six years on Tour I was consistently one of the top four or five putters out there. I just wish I could putt that well now. (In 1992 I was 142nd on the PGA Tour's putting statistics list, and in 1993, 129th. Stan, where are you?)

Stan also helped me through the maturing process from being a good college player to playing the Tour itself. He advised me about handling things like travel and adjusting to different courses in varying regions, and generally helped me learn everything it takes to become a competent professional.

At this point I should credit a fourth individual— Jack Bell—a golf pro who put a little fire in my belly during my college days and generally helped me improve the mental side of my game. Bell, formerly from the Chicago area, came to La Jolla and immediately took an interest in my game. In fact, it was Bell's intelligent tutoring that had a lot to do with my winning the 1973 U.S. Amateur, which was played at Inverness in Toledo, Ohio, a great old course that later also hosted the U.S. Open and the PGA Championship.

In the days leading up to my departure to the Amateur, I was practicing at La Jolla with Jack observing. Afterward he told me, "Kid, when you get out to Inverness, you aren't going to know anybody. Nobody's going to know you or care at all about you either. If you want to make friends with somebody after a round, fine. But when you're on that golf course, there's only one thing you're there for, and that's to beat the hell out of everybody else. You've got all the game you need to do it. So go do it!"

Of course, I'd been looking forward to the Amateur and thought I could make a good showing. But Jack's hard-line pep talk was, I think, a watershed mark in my golfing career. Up to that point I'd never been completely focused on what I wanted to accomplish. But I was definitely in the zone at Inverness, from first tee shot to final putt. In the quarter-finals I beat Dick Siderowf, the British Amateur champion, 2 and 1. Then, in the semifinal, I upset Vinny Giles, a renowned amateur and the defending champion, 3 and 1. Finally, I knocked off David Strawn by a 6 and 5 margin to take the title. I had become the U.S. Amateur champion before the start of my junior year in college.

With that victory came the realization that I had the game to become a Tour player. I'm glad, though, that I stayed at USC for two more years, honing my game and becoming more consistent. I was named an All-American in both 1974 and 1975, and playing for the U.S. in the 1975 Walker Cup, won all three of my matches. Even with that additional experience and preparation time, though, my early days on the PGA Tour were far from a piece of cake.

A DROWNING WALRUS

After graduating from USC in 1975, I turned pro and went to the PGA Tour Qualifying School that fall. There, despite all my recent successes, came a shocker—I failed to qualify for my tour card.

Actually, I was pretty fortunate. Back then, there were two qualifying schools per year, in spring and fall. That meant I got to try again the following spring, at which time I made it. So I started playing the Tour during the second half of 1976.

The early results were pathetic. I played like a bum and was pretty much living like one, too, seeing as how I earned only $2,702 in official money for the rest of that season. At that point I was as far away from being a good player, to say nothing of a leading money winner and a major championship winner, as anyone who ever came down the pike.

Everybody goes through a period where things aren't going anywhere near like they had hoped. That's how it was for me in 1976. That year I learned the hard way how high the standard of golf is on the PGA Tour. The difference is like night and day compared to the college or amateur circuits. There I would enter a tournament knowing that only a handful of players had a chance to beat me. On Tour I was just one of 150 top-notch players. All of them were capable of beating me like a drum on any given day, particularly since I was an inexperienced rookie.

After a veteran has played in a particular event three or four times, he feels pretty comfortable. He knows what hotels to stay in, the best route to the course, the best places to eat, where to get his clothes cleaned. But mainly, he understands the golf course intimately. He knows its trouble spots, he knows where he can gamble, he knows how the wind usually blows, and he knows all the subtle breaks in the greens that the rookie hasn't deciphered yet. If you add up all this knowledge the veteran has, I'd say that over the course of a 72-hole tournament, he's got about a four-shot edge over the first-timer.

I realized I'd had all these factors working against me in the first go-round. But I knew I had to start swinging the club better too. For that reason I practiced harder than ever prior to the start of the 1977 PGA Tour season.

Things didn't turn around all at once—they seldom do—but in 1977 I started to make the 36-hole cuts and then to throw in an occasional high finish. For the year I finished sixty-sixth on the money list with $42,949. That sounds like chicken feed—heck, nowadays a pro can win that much by coming in fifth in a single tournament. But at that stage I was delighted to have it, along with the knowledge that my hard work on the practice tee was starting to pay off.

THE WALRUS TAKES A WIFE

The next couple of years were experience gainers in which I didn't win any official tournaments (although I did win the 1978 Magnolia Classic, the unofficial event then played the same week as the Masters). There was another big adjustment that occurred during that time. I married my girlfriend Sue in January 1979. It was one of the best moves I ever made. Sue has had a huge, positive influence on my career. She is by far my biggest fan, but she can also be my harshest critic. She knows when to encourage me and when I need a swift kick in the butt to get me back out on the practice tee.

When she does that, by the way, I don't immediately appreciate it. After all, like most blue-collar guys, I have a tendency to want to kick back and watch some weekend sports with a supply of brews in hand. But after she's done it, I always have to admit that that kick in the rear was both necessary and very well timed.

Sue has always been a trouper in terms of adjusting to traveling on the Tour or being home alone. It was especially rough when our two boys were little tykes (Kevin was born early in 1980; Chris, late in 1982). But Sue has never complained. She's a big factor in any success I've had.

THE WALRUS CATCHES SOME BIG FISH

Everything came together for me in the years from 1980 through 1984. My long game had become much more consistent; I was putting very well, and I had gotten the feel of being in contention a few times. I broke through to win the Bob Hope Desert Classic in Palm Springs early in 1980, and followed it up with a win at Greensboro a couple of months later. After getting over that major hump, I felt like anything was possible. Sure, I would still have my bad weeks, but when I did I honestly believed I could turn it around at any time and win again.

Over that five-year period from 1980 through 1984, I won eight official Tour events, including one major (the 1982 Masters). I was the Tour's leading money winner in 1982 when I claimed four events, and finished among the top ten on the money list in four of those five years. My worst year in that stretch was 1983, when I finished seventeenth on the money list.

The cake, of course, was my Masters victory in

I AM THE WALRUS

1982. In retrospect, I took advantage of an especially great opportunity to snare one of the most cherished prizes in the game. The reason I say that is, the weather that year in Augusta was alternately rainy or windy. That's good for me because I've always been a good bad-weather player. Stronger players like me have an edge when it's wet and you need to carry the ball. And I've always been a pretty good wind player. I think the reason is that I'm fairly short and, ahem, a little bit heavyset (240 pounds). So I don't get jostled by the wind as much as the slighter, flat-bellied players (which is just about everybody). And there's not a lot of lower-body movement in my swing to begin with, which also helps. I can hit it solid in the wind.

Anyhow, that year at Augusta was a nightmare for a lot of players. The Masters tournament committee had decided to speed up the already fast, sloping greens. The practice days prior to the event had been windy and cold, and these conditions made the greens fast beyond belief. It was nothing to putt a ball clear off the green. Everybody was thinking that 300, or twelve *over* par, would be a good score.

Things changed drastically when the tournament began on Thursday. We played the opening round in a cold, hard, driving rain. This would soften the greens some for later in the week, and eventually help the scoring. But that first round was murder, the toughest weather I've played in at Augusta. I shot a three-over-par 75. When I came in, I was wet, cold, and disappointed with my score. As the other players finished, though, I started to realize something—my 75 wasn't all that bad.

Craig Stadler

The second day, the storm had passed through but it was windy and cold, so the course still played really tough. I shot a solid 69 and, at even par 144, was tied for the lead with Curtis Strange.

Saturday is known on Tour as "moving day," the day the pros play more aggressively in order to move into potential tournament-winning positions. On this particular Saturday I definitely moved in the right direction. I shot a five-under-par 67, highlighted by long birdie putts on the last three holes. When all the scores were in, I led the Masters by three shots. One more strong round and the Walrus would be clad in green.

Going into that final day, I felt pretty calm and in control. I think it's to my advantage that I don't put the major titles on a pedestal, way above all the other events. This way, the final-day choke factor at a major isn't much greater than normal. (But a choke factor still exists, believe me. Any player who tells you he's never choked is full of bull.)

Most of that final day, though, I was cruising. After eleven holes I was three-under for the day, eight-under for the championship, and had a six-shot lead. Then the Chinese fire drill started.

I don't think what transpired on the closing holes was an out-and-out choke on my part. Over what was to become an agonizing final stretch, I stayed pretty calm and didn't throw any fits. Although nerves might have played a part, I think it was more that the great Augusta National course caught up with me. Without hitting any really bad shots, I bogeyed holes twelve, fourteen, sixteen, and eighteen, three-putting the last. That gave me a 73 for the round and a 284 total. Meanwhile, Dan Pohl shot a strong 67, and we finished in a tie.

I barely had time to check and sign my scorecard before we were whisked back to the tenth hole to start a sudden-death play-off.

The play-off was sort of anticlimactic. I made a solid par four on this left-twisting, downhill 485-yarder—good drive, good six-iron, two putts from forty feet. Dan missed the green right and wound up needing a ten-footer to tie me. He just missed it. Lo and behold, a Walrus in a green jacket!

THE VETERAN WALRUS

The second half of the 1980s was not as kind to me as the first half had been. Although my official Tour earnings totaled $1.4 million over that stretch, I didn't win a single U.S. event. I did win the 1985 European Masters and the 1987 Dunlop Phoenix in Japan, however, so the cupboard wasn't exactly bare.

In a sense, I think the problems I encountered during the mid-to-late eighties were to some extent a case of my "outsmarting" myself a little bit. I'd always been a natural type of player, a feel player. I was always aware of what I could do and what I couldn't do, and I played to my strengths. But by then, I was a Masters champion and a leading money winner, and I began to think maybe I ought to have *all* the shots down pat.

I think a turning point came early in 1985. At the Bob Hope Desert Classic, which I'd won five years earlier, I played a heck of a tournament and wound up in a play-off for the title. That first play-off hole did not set up well for me. It called for a draw off the tee and my bread-and-butter shot was a power fade. At any rate, I tried to hit a draw there, hung the ball out into the garbage on the right, made bogey, and was out of the play-off.

That failure to hit the right-to-left shot on demand really stuck in my craw. I became more aware of the times throughout the season when having a draw in my bag would have helped. So in the next off-season I decided to reverse my tendencies and become a right-to-left player. I also talked myself into reasoning that as I got older, the slightly greater distance a draw provided would help me too.

I played the 1986 season predominantly drawing (or trying to draw) my full shots. To make a long story short, I had my worst season since 1979, particularly in the consistency of my ball striking. And I finished a mediocre fifty-third on the money list.

The following season I started working with Dick Harmon of the River Oaks Country Club, in Houston. Dick taught me how to hit a controlled draw, so that I could play it confidently when I had to. However, we came to the conclusion that my best move would be to go back to my old left-to-right shot and use it almost always. After all, I'd won the Masters with a left-to-right game, on a course where everyone says you have to be able to hit a hard hook to win.

Once I made this decision, I began hitting the ball well again. The wins were hard to come by, but mainly because my putting wasn't quite on the same level as it had been in my first few pro seasons.

I AM THE WALRUS

Folks, I think there's a good lesson in this for you. If you're a weekend player and don't get to work on your game as much as you'd like (we'll be addressing that point in detail in Chapter Two), you're probably better off relying on what you do best than trying to hit every type of shot perfectly. Because that's what I tried to do, and I had all the time in the world to work on it. And it didn't work.

Learn from my experience. If you're already playing respectable golf, unless you have the time to put in a complete overhaul of your game, don't stray too far from what comes naturally to you. Certainly, if you're consistently shooting over 100 and have no idea what kind of shot you'll hit next, you need to make some fundamental swing changes. But if you have one type of shot you can rely on, even if it's not a pretty shot, hang on to it. They don't give you any style points in this game.

The last few seasons, since 1990, have represented a renaissance in my career. Thanks to the explosive growth of the purses we compete for, I've continued to bank bigger and bigger checks. More important, from my perspective, I've won three more Tour events so far in the nineties (plus the 1990 Scandinavian Open). Winning the 1991 Tour Championship at Pinehurst's *Number Two* course, in North Carolina, brought me my single biggest paycheck ever, $360,000, and vaulted me into second place on the money list. The victory also qualified me for the 1992 World Series of Golf—and I won that title too! In early 1994, I claimed a very satisfying victory by winning the Buick Invitational in my old hometown of San Diego.

Craig Stadler

THE WALRUS'S BIGGEST DISAPPOINTMENTS

Though I've had a very satisfying career, it has not come without some disappointments. Every good player out here carries with him a few horror stories about how he let a championship get away. Actually, the better the player, the more horror stories he's likely to have, because it means the player has been in contention a lot.

What's so tough about the Tour is that there's only one winner every week. Out of 150 or more very talented players in any tournament field, only one guy can be the top dog. Even though some of the also-rans make a big check, they are still also-rans.

I think it's fair to say that anyone who finished in the top ten in any tournament can realistically look back at a couple of things that went against him that would have made the difference. So you have a lot more high finishers walking around talking to themselves than you do tournament winners.

As for me, I haven't let too many of the losses wear down my mental resolve. If I play well but don't win, I tell myself, "Hey, you had a great week. You're playing well. Just keep doing what you're doing and your turn will come soon." Still, I admit that some losses are harder to recover from than others.

Most of you probably think that losses in the major championships would always be the ones that hurt the most. For example, many golf historians point to Arnold Palmer's shocking loss to Billy Casper in the 1966 U.S. Open (when he blew a seven-stroke lead with nine holes to play) as the turning point in his great career. To me, though, any tournament loss can be upsetting, depending on the circumstances.

There's one tournament I absolutely, positively threw away—just gave it to the winner. That was the 1990 Hawaiian Open at Waialae Country Club, won by David Ishii. This is definitely not meant to put down David Ishii, who had a terrific week. But this is what happened during the final round. I kept hitting the ball close to the hole—ten feet, eight feet, five feet, always close. Sadly though, I missed birdie putt after birdie putt. I've never hit the ball so well and putted so atrociously in the same round. To top it off, I three-putted the eighteenth green to drop into a tie for second, two strokes behind the winner. Folks, if I had putted even decently that day, I'd have won that Hawaiian Open by five or six shots. A breeze.

I think that Hawaiian Open was significant because, even though I hadn't putted very well for a while before then, this loss really brought my putting woes to a head. Now, unfortunately, I know I can lose at any time. Sometimes it's better *not* to have a lot of experience, I guess.

My second biggest disappointment came when I played in my first Masters, in 1979. (As you may recall, in 1978 I'd won the unofficial Magnolia Classic. That qualified me to go to Augusta the next year. Well, even for a laid-back golfer like myself, playing in my first Masters was an experience I'll never forget. When I made that drive down Magnolia Lane, I couldn't help but say to myself, "Wow, I have arrived as a genuine entity in the game of golf.")

To shorten a long and painful story, I managed to overcome a few early jitters, and as the week progressed, moved up the leader board. By the seventh hole of the final round, I was tied for the lead. And, although I tried to fight it off, a tiny voice inside my head started whispering, "You can win this thing." I tried to fight that little voice off, but I couldn't. And that was the beginning of the end.

I bogeyed the par-five eighth, got a little rattled, and fell apart during the famous stretch of holes at Augusta that ends with the diabolical par-three twelfth. I think I played numbers eight through twelve in six- or seven-over-par. I remember I was almost in tears on the thirteenth tee when I realized I couldn't possibly win.

Maybe I wouldn't have won that Masters even if I'd kept my composure. Regardless, that loss was a hard lesson in patience and not thinking ahead, but it was a *good lesson*.

My third greatest disappointment definitely occurred during my first visit to the Canadian Open, which I believe was in 1977. That's when I found out that at the Canadian Open *they don't sell beer on Sundays!* Man, I can't tell you what a crushing blow that was. There's nothing I like better, once my final round is finished and a hard week's work done, than to retreat to the grill or locker room with a substantial flow of my favorite lager. You just can't do it at the Canadian Open. Truly, the sacrifices of being a PGA Tour player are high.

You know I'm only kidding, of course. There's no

career I could ever imagine that could hold a candle to what I've experienced over nearly twenty years of competition.

Sometimes fans or friends ask me what I would have done if I hadn't made it on the Tour. That's a good question. Most people could probably envision me right at home behind the wheel of a giant rig on Route 66. But believe it or not, I really don't think I would have ended up being a trucker. In college I majored in math, and at the time enjoyed learning about the stock market. So I think there's a good chance I would have explored being a stockbroker if I'd ever had to get a real job. How about a Walrus in a pin-striped suit? It could have happened. Then I'd have ended up playing in a regular weekend foursome rather than battling all the "flat bellies" on the Tour.

At times I've imagined an ideal foursome. Here's who it would consist of besides myself: 1) My son Kevin, because I'm proud to watch his game develop; 2) Rush Limbaugh, not necessarily for his opinions but because he weighs more than me; and 3) Konishiki, the sumo wrestler who not only tips but breaks the scales at something like 500 pounds.

Now that you know a little more about me, let's take a walk out to the practice tee and see what we can do to make you, the blue-collar golfer, a better player—and to have a blast at the same time.

2
PRACTICE, PRACTICE, PRACTICE:

How to Have Fun While Mastering Golf's Scoring Shots

As the top-ranking blue-collar golfer on the PGA Tour, I think I have a clear understanding of most blue-collar, weekend golfers' attitudes toward golf practice. Basically, you can't stand it and don't want to know about it. "Look," you might say, "I work five days a week for eight or ten hours a day. I don't want to work on my golf game too. With my limited free time, I want to *play* golf. Nobody's going to convince me to become a slave to the practice tee."

Well, I'd like to say something here that's probably going to surprise you. At this point in my career I don't like to practice a whole lot either. When I'm not on the Tour, I like to get away from time to time and enjoy other activities, such as being with my family, hunting, skiing, or watching the L.A. Kings. Even when I'm working on my game, I hate the idea of lugging one of those big metal baskets that holds maybe four hundred balls out to the practice tee, then standing there thinking, "Now I've got to hit all of these for the next four or five hours." Unless you're the second coming of Ben Hogan or maybe Tom Kite, let's face it, beating several hundred balls is not a very appealing thought.

So I'm going to say something here that might inspire you to actually read this chapter and consider what I have to offer. I don't think that you have to hit balls for hours on end in order to have a meaningful practice. Instead, I'd like to convince you that practice can actually be fun.

The kind of practice I'm talking about, though, is very thorough, well-rounded, and goes far beyond just beating balls. I'm going to suggest you start taking a whole new approach toward improving your game, by employing the three *E*'s of good practice. That is, learn to practice *eagerly, efficiently,* and *enjoyably*. If you understand what this type of practice entails, I think you'll agree it's well worth doing.

AVOID UNREAL EXPECTATIONS

Always remember this: It's not the quantity of your practice that counts, but the quality.

I've noticed that many amateurs who are willing to practice have an unrealistic attitude about what practice should do for them. Often they equate hitting drives with improving. They figure if they've hit a thousand balls in a given week, it means they should automatically improve, immediately! If they shoot the same scores after they've practiced a lot, they're disappointed (and may decide it's not worth it to practice in the future).

Let me level with you: there are no guarantees in this game. Anybody who believes that they'll automatically play better by hitting range balls all day long is thinking foolishly. The game of golf is far more complex than that. You can't equate how many range balls you've hit with how much progress you'll make.

Good practice, in my opinion, doesn't require you to hit as many balls as you might think. However, it does require you to make every practice shot you hit a *smart* practice shot. So, now, I'd like to show you what I mean by practicing intelligently.

BE EAGER TO IMPROVE

What do you enjoy most about the game of golf?

There are a lot of reasonable answers to this question. Among them are getting exercise, being with friends, being in the outdoors, and just enjoying recreation after a long workweek. But I'll bet that deep down, many of you enjoy golf as a form of competition, and that improving and shooting lower scores is one of the main attractions of the game. Is that true for you? If it is, if you're truly eager to improve, you've got to commit yourself to practicing smart every chance you get.

Sure, I know, you've got the responsibilities of a job, family, chores at home, and so on. It's not like you can say, "I think I'll take the day off and put in some really hard work on my game." No, at least during the workweek, that's not going to happen. But let's think a little bit about what you *can* do.

Craig Stadler

Let's say you usually play one round each weekend during the playing season, two if you're lucky. That's about fifty rounds of golf per year. You almost never touch a club during the week. This amount of play is probably just enough to keep your game at about the same level all the time. Unfortunately, unless you're an outstanding athlete, you don't have a realistic chance to improve unless you can work on your game some more.

So ask yourself, "How can I get in a little more work on my game?" You don't have to be a martyr and force yourself to hit balls for three hours after work even though you're exhausted. What I'm asking is, can you practice for one hour after work, one weekday per week? Can you practice twice during the week? If you can't spare a full hour, can you practice twice a week, for forty to forty-five minutes each time? Maybe it means missing the evening news or just reading the paper a little later two nights a week.

If you're truly eager to improve, I'll bet you'll find you can get in at least two forty-five-minute practice sessions per week. If you can do more, that's great. But my point is to make use of those little blocks of time that you do have. It's far better to put in frequent, short practice sessions than it is to occasionally force yourself into a long, tiring one, or not to practice at all.

Even if you can't go to the range or the course for a short practice, there are still things you can do whenever you have ten or fifteen minutes free. How about slowly swinging a weighted golf club on a weekday evening, just to keep your golfing muscles toned up? If you have a backyard, why not take your sand wedge outside and practice some little flip shots? Make it fun—try to pop the ball over obstacles such as an above-ground swimming pool or a bush, and land it in a designated area.

You know, I think one reason I'm a very good wedge player is that in my teens, I worked at the driving range at La Jolla, picking up balls. I'd always have a wedge with me, gathering balls that were in nooks and crannies around the edges of the range, finding balls in deep grass and hitting them out over fences, bushes, and the like. Handling that wedge so much really paid off over time.

When the weather's bad, how about stroking some putts in your den or living room? Again, make it fun. Practice hitting ten-foot putts toward a small target like a quarter or a book of matches. Keep score. How many can you "make" out of ten?

These are the little ways you can learn to work on your game even when your time is limited. If you're eager to practice and improve, your efforts will start paying off sooner than you think.

MAKE YOUR PRACTICE EFFICIENT

Since we already know your practice time is limited, let's talk about seven ways to make the time you can spend on your game as efficient as possible.

1. Stay in Touch with a Teacher. My first recommendation to you, the handicap player, regards the full swing. You should find a teacher in your area with a reputation for giving sound instruction, and invest in a lesson or two. The reason I say this is that golfers can't see themselves swing. Most amateurs, and even many pros, aren't actually doing what they think they're doing in executing the golf swing.

I know, I know, you may not have much time or money to spend on lessons. But how about checking in with a good local teaching pro at the beginning of each new season? This way you can make sure that your fundamentals—grip, address position, posture, balance—are in good shape, and that you haven't picked up any bad habits in the past year.

I'd also recommend that if at any time during the season you run into a bad streak and can't figure out what you're doing differently, see your pro if at all possible. He or she may save you a lot of practice time you'd have wasted by ingraining poor setup and/or swing habits.

You might think that, as long as I've played on the tour, I pretty much can take care of my own swing. Usually that's true. However, there are times when I just can't seem to hit the ball the way I want. That's why I go down to River Oaks Country Club in Houston and see Dick Harmon maybe four or five times a year. Dick knows my swing and knows what to look for. He saves me not only time in determining what the problem is, but also keeps me from making any false moves in correcting my swing that will get me in deeper trouble. If at all possible, keep in touch with one person you can trust with your swing.

2. Always Loosen Up Before Practicing.This advice is good for everyone, but particularly for the blue-collar golfer who, to put it mildly, is not quite in tip-top condition.

Of course, it would look pretty foolish for me to

advise you to get in great shape to play golf, when I've been carrying around an extra thirty pounds of fat for most of my career. However, everyone should take a couple of minutes to loosen up their joints before hitting any full practice shots, to avoid muscle pulls and strains that can disrupt your game or put you on the sidelines temporarily. Here's the simplest exercise I know of for loosening up those vital golf muscles involved in swinging a club:

Grasp a club with one hand near each end of the shaft and raise it over your head. Then do side bends in both directions, holding your position rather than bouncing.

3. Have a Specific Purpose for Every Shot You Hit. Don't ever hit a practice shot without knowing the exact purpose for it. Always have a specific target on the range in mind. Decide if you want to hit a straight shot to that target, or if you'd like to draw it, fade it, hit it high and soft, or hit a low punch. Whatever the type of shot you envision, decide on one specific "swing thought" that will help you make that shot come off. Don't clutter your mind with a bunch of different mechanical thoughts. Stick with one key—for example, "low and slow back," or "full turn around the spine," or "steady head."

Last, take your time with each shot. Get a clear picture of the shot you have in mind before you step up to each ball. Even if you don't have much time to practice, you'll be a lot better off if you hit well-planned shots instead of rushed ones.

4. Work on Your Weakest Club. Most players have a tendency to hit their favorite club most fre-

This side-bend exercise is one of the best for limbering up those vital muscles involved in the golf swing.

quently on the driving range, and leave their problem clubs in the bag. Or, if their favorite shot is a draw, they'll just practice a nice draw and never try to do what they're weak at—hitting it straight or fading it.

If you know where you're losing strokes on the course, commit most of your practice time to your weak points. If your long irons are troubling you and you have to play a lot of them on your home course, hit them more often, keeping a singular swing key in mind. If your long putting has been letting you down, spend more time on the practice green working on controlling your speed.

5. *Compartmentalize Your Practice.* If you have plenty of time for a nice long practice session, you can and should cover all aspects—short game shots, putting, iron play, tee shots. More often, as we've discussed, you're going to be fitting in short practice sessions when you can. If this is the case, it's a good idea to compartmentalize your practice.

Say you can get in two forty-five-minute sessions during the week. In the first of those two sessions practice your full shots; devote the next session to your short game and putting. If you try to work on both full swing and short game in one forty-five-minute session, you really won't have time to get in a rhythm with your full swing. Taking your time, as I recommended, you'd only be able to hit thirty balls or so, and the tendency would be to start rushing your shots rather than planning and visualizing them. Instead, use the whole forty-five minutes to hit at least sixty full shots, with several different clubs.

If it's your day to practice the short game, spend just about half your time on greenside chips, short pitches, and definitely on bunker play, if a practice bunker is available. (The majority of amateurs fear the sand, and the main reason is most of them never practice from it. If the weekender could hit even ten or fifteen bunker shots during the short game practice, it wouldn't take long before he or she got enough familiarity with the shot to play it reasonably well.) Finally, spend the other twenty to twenty-five minutes on the green itself, using one or more of the games we'll talk about shortly.

6. *Keep It Simple.* Many weekenders get caught up in trying out new tips every time they go to the practice tee. Someone in your foursome tells you about a move that's been working for him, and you figure it's got to help you, so you'll try it too.

Let me advise you right now to stick with the basics when you're on the practice tee. That tip you heard about probably won't even last a week for your playing companion. Why should you chance fouling yourself up with any piecemeal ideas?

There really aren't too many tricks in the golf swing. Stick with the basics, even if you hit a few bad shots. Don't consider any major changes unless you're in a slump. If that does happen, you should go to your teaching pro for a closer examination.

7. *Groove a Rhythmic Swing.* Everybody talks about keeping a smooth tempo. But how many players manage this when they're on the practice tee? Usually by the end of a session, they're banging the driver and swinging twice as hard as they were when they started. Poor shots are the result.

Here's a suggestion. If you're only hitting, say, sixty balls, hit them with various clubs in the following order:

Number of Balls	Club
12	Pitching wedge
12	3-iron
12	7-iron
12	Driver
12	5-iron

You can alter club selection, of course, as long as you make sure to *go from a short club to a long club, back to a shorter club, then to a long club, then finish with a middle iron.* Always start with some easy wedge shots to loosen up and get that smooth, easy rhythm established. Then maintain that same rhythm with the rest of your practice clubs.

MAKE YOUR PRACTICE ENJOYABLE

In any type of endeavor, a person will accomplish an awful lot more if they enjoy what they're doing. I think that's especially true of your practice time. If you're not looking forward to practicing, you might as well not bother.

No one can make you want to work to improve your game. However, there are lots of ways to make practice sessions fun while at the same time making them as productive as possible. How can you accomplish this? By making practice as much like a golf round as possible. After all, you like to play golf, don't you?

Basically, what you need to do is play games with yourself. You've got to use your imagination to create specific, real situations that you'd also encounter on the golf course. Then try to execute each shot that you've pictured in your mind's eye.

You might be thinking that this imagination stuff sounds pretty childish—like when you were a kid and you said to yourself, "This putt's for the U.S. Open." That's exactly the way I want you to approach your practice shots. You don't have to tell yourself every shot's for the U.S. Open, but in your mind's eye you should approach each shot just like you would the ones you face on the course.

I once read in a newspaper about a college football coach who was getting a new quarterback ready for the upcoming season. When the offense was in the huddle during practice scrimmages, the coach wouldn't just tell the quarterback to run a draw play or throw a sideline pass. The coach would present the quarterback with a complete game situation. For example, he'd tell him to imagine it was third down and five to go, thc ball was on the opponents' 45-yard line, there were two minutes to go, and the score was tied. Then the coach would tell the quarterback to choose the play. Do you see how much more vivid a learning experience this would be for the player? When the real game started, no matter what the situation, the quarterback would feel as though he'd been there before. He'd have a good idea what would work, what wouldn't, and why.

This is exactly the type of approach you should

take with your practice sessions. Imagine a tough situation. Put some pressure on yourself. I guarantee that if you use your imagination, your practice sessions will never feel dull. In fact, you'll probably find yourself running over your practice time limit.

On the following pages I'd like to list some ways you can make all aspects of your practice much more enjoyable and much more productive.

1. *Practice on the Golf Course.* If the opportunity exists, the best way to practice is to do so on the actual "playing field." I realize this may be difficult, particularly if you play at a public course. But often you can get a hole or two to yourself for a little while before twilight.

Do the following: Let's assume you're on the tee of a par four that's relatively open down the left side, but has woods or other trouble on the right. However, your best shot into the green is from the right side of the fairway. Hit several tee shots. Try to hit one in the right side of the fairway, one to the left side, and one down the middle. How successful were these tee shots? Did you feel comfortable trying to hit the portion of the fairway nearest the trouble? If so, great. However, if you felt more confident aiming down the middle, you've learned something about your mental approach. Maybe you'll find you want to steer away from the trouble completely by aiming left. Finally, consider this: Was the driver the right club to hit to this fairway?

When you get out to the landing area, toss three balls down on the fairway: one in the middle, one on the left side, one on the right side. Play all three shots to the green. Was the shot in from the right

During your on-course practice sessions, hit several drives to see which shot you're most comfortable with.

side of the fairway so much simpler that it's worth the risk to try to hit your tee shot there? Or would you rather play safer from the tee and accept a tougher second shot?

Next, play a couple of short approach shots from bad lies in the rough. Seeing how many real-life shots must be played from the deep grass, it's wise to work on them.

The drawings show this type of lie and how to play the shot. From deep rough, position the ball farther back in the stance than normal, toward your right foot. With the ball in this position, you're almost forced to swing the clubhead down into the ball on a steep arc. This allows you to hit the ball first, before the clubhead is slowed by the rough.

Next, hit a couple of trouble shots from the woods. How small an opening are you confident you can thread your ball through? Is it worth trying to go for the green or is it smarter to pitch out? (By the way, when you're practicing from trees, *always* go for it! You need to find out whether you should go for it or play safe when you find a similar situation in the future.)

When you get near the green, play a variety of pitch shots from the fairway grass. Then determine the easiest place to save par from if you do miss the green with your approach. That way, when you play the course, you'll know where not to hit the ball.

If there's no practice bunker at your local golf facility, go out on the course to hone your sand game. Take a couple of balls and flip them in a bunker so they're sitting reasonably well. Make your normal sand shot swing (we'll discuss the shot in detail in

When practicing from a bad lie in rough (top), set up with the ball back in your stance (left), since this address position encourages you to deliver the club sharply into the ball (right).

Chapter Three) and observe how the ball comes out. Play a game with yourself based on your current expertise from the sand. How often can you stop the ball within ten feet of the cup? Or within twenty feet?

While practicing sand shots, you should also brush up on those semiburied "fried egg" lies we all know and love. As we'll see later, you'll need to adjust your technique, squaring the blade to help it get under the ball. Watch how the ball comes out of this lie "hotter" than when the lie is good. It will have almost no backspin and thus will run upon landing. Make a note to plan for this extra run the next time you have such a shot in actual play.

I think playing these on-the-course games is the best type of practicing you can do. Try it.

The rest of these practice techniques assume you're at the practice tee or the practice putting green.

2. Practice Controlled Tee Shots. Don't just whale at the driver, trying to hit it farther than the guy next to you. Instead, compete with yourself. Hit a series of tee shots, and keep score of how many fairways out of fourteen you can hit in an imaginary round. (Keep in mind that there will usually be four par-three holes on the course.)

In your mind's eye, draw a fairway on the practice tee that's thirty-five to forty yards wide. (Use some type of marker to identify each edge of the fairway, such as a fairway flag or the line to a lone tree in the distance.) What's your personal best for fairways hit in regulation? Always try to beat your previous record to put some pressure on yourself and simulate the course situation.

When you practice your tee shots in this manner, you may find you're automatically making a smoother and more balanced swing, and making better contact. That's because your goal has changed from swinging aggressively to hitting the ball in the fairway.

Incidentally, this fairways-in-regulation practice may be an eye-opener to you. The straightest drivers on the PGA Tour hit only between 75 and 80 percent of the fairways. That means they hit about eleven out of fourteen fairways per round.

Almost all amateurs hit the ball in the fairway far less than they think they do. You may find that you're currently hitting only one third of your tee shots in the fairway, or even fewer. If so, you'll know that you should devote more of your future practice time to your driving.

3. *If You're Driving It Straight, Up the Ante.* If you're hitting a lot of fairways (say two thirds or more), challenge yourself with your next row of teed-up balls. Try to hit one side of the fairway with the first ball, the opposite side of the fairway with the next. Keep track of how many balls in succession you can hit into the preferred side of the fairway.

Another advanced tee shot drill is to try to hit the ball in the fairway with a fade, then try to do it with a draw, alternating each time. How many can you hit in the fairway each way? With which type of shot do you tend to hit the fairway more often? This is great information to know for future rounds. Also, alternating draws and fades is a great way for the more advanced player to fine-tune the feel of a controlled swing.

4. *Target Your Iron Shots.* There are a couple of useful and fun methods of homing in on a target when practicing your irons. One is to pick out a specific target on the practice area, then try to see how many balls out of ten you can hit within a predetermined circle, which constitutes a successful result. For example, once you've picked out your target, compete with yourself to find out how many nine-iron shots you can hit within a circle twenty feet around the target. Later, pick out another target, and see how many five-iron shots out of ten you can put within thirty feet.

Your goals will vary according to your skill level, so make your target range realistic. Try to give yourself a range that's fairly difficult with each club, but not so hard that you can't hit any shots within it. Keep working toward improving on your personal best. If you get to a point where you're regularly hitting seven or eight out of ten shots inside the circle, great! Then reduce the size of your good-shot circle and try to improve some more.

One last point regarding this target drill: Pick a spot for a target that's easily within a given club's range. You don't want to start forcing shots with any club.

There's another way of targeting your iron game that's even more realistic. Envision, in succession, the approach shots from the fairway (or the tee on par-three holes) to each of the eighteen holes on your home course. Play each shot as if you're on the course. If on the first hole your average drive would leave you a six-iron to the green, take out that club and play the shot. If the next hole would call for a five-wood, use that, and so on. You know the configuration of every green on the course, so you can pretty well judge whether each shot would have hit the green or not. Keep track of your score and always aim to beat it.

5. *What's Your Chipping Score?* I think I enjoy chipping more than anything else. Maybe because you know that when you get the ball "up and down," in a sense you've saved a stroke—gotten one back from the course, if you will. And holing out a chip is even better.

Set up your chip shots with the ball positioned just ahead of center in your stance and your feet close together. Grip down on the handle slightly to enhance your control. Make sure the leading edge of your blade is pointed right on line to where you must land the ball in order for it to take any break as it runs to the cup.

Practice short, lofted chips with a wedge, and longer, more running ones with a six-, seven-, or eight-iron. With each club, hit ten chips. Keep score as follows: Every time your ball finishes within three feet of the cup, give yourself a point. If you hole one out, score five points. What's your personal best point total? Always try to beat it the next time.

6. *Make Short Putting Your Armor.* Have you ever stopped to think how many strokes you lose on short putts of, say, four feet or less? When you blow one of those, unlike miscues from the tee or on the approach, that shot's gone forever. It can't be recovered. The ability to make short putts can accurately be called your last line of defense as a golfer.

You're wise if you spend the majority of your putting practice drilling yourself to become a rock-solid holer of short putts. You've got to have confidence that you're going to make these little "knee knockers." In fact, I'll go so far as to say you shouldn't just have confidence that it's going in. You have to *know* every short putt is going in, just as sure as the sun's coming up again tomorrow.

Keep your backswing short when practicing short, lofted chip shots with a wedge.

Craig Stadler

Well, you might think that's easier said than done. And I admit, you're going to have to work at it. But I want to help you work on your short putting the right way, and at the same time, make it fun so you'll keep working at it. Here's what to do.

First, make sure your alignment is sound. Start with some short putts that are dead straight. Have a friend check your putterblade closely at address, to confirm that your alignment is perfect. I'm not really dogmatic about how your putting setup should look, except that the blade is square and that you are in a solid, comfortable position.

The keys to making short putts are to have perfect alignment and to stay as still as possible when executing the stroke. There are no tricks to the stroke itself, especially one that's as brief as this one will be. Trust your instincts to draw the putterblade back and through with the proper distance and with the correct force for this particular putt. Keep your head as still as if it were in a vise until the stroke is completed. If you can only keep your head still, you'll make a very high percentage of the short ones.

Stroke your short putts solidly into the back of the cup—don't "wish" them in. If you take this approach, you'll find you can play most of the short ones straight or very close to straight—they won't have time to break much.

Now let's get to the fun part of short putting. Here are two games that should really give your confidence a boost. First, drop a few balls three feet from the cup. See how many in a row you can make. It may take you a few rolls to get your alignment and stroke just right, but if you follow the simple mechanics described, I'll bet you start running off a nice string of holed putts. Surely you can hole ten three-footers in a row. How about twenty? Note your personal best and always aim to beat it. As an incentive, promise yourself a "cold one" every time you break your record.

This is great practice because once you get on a roll, you'll be reinforcing your subconscious with the repetitive, positive image of the ball going into the hole.

It won't be long before you reach a point where you're saying to yourself, "This is boring. I'll make every one of these." If that happens, then make the short-putt game a little tougher by playing the left-right game. It's simple. From three feet, knock your first putt into the left side of the cup. After you do this, sink your next putt into the right side of the cup. Continue to alternate sides.

In effect, your target is now half the size of a regular hole. Can you alternate left and right and make ten in a row? If so, congratulations—you're becoming a rock-solid short putter. Incidentally, you'll be able to check whether you've made the putt into the correct side of the hole without moving your head. Since the hole is only three feet away, you'll be able to see it with your peripheral vision, without actually moving.

Believe me, this is the best practice putting you can do. When you become a superconfident short putter, you'll find yourself becoming more proficient on medium and long putts too. The reason is that your outlook will be more positive and you'll become a bit more aggressive in your stroke. You'll know you're not going to three-putt. If you run your first one a touch by the hole, the come-backer is no problem, right? Net result: You hole some of the longer ones too.

PRACTICE IN YOUR ARMCHAIR

Now we come to the most enjoyable part of practice. This is the kind done in the comfort of your home. I usually do it sitting in my favorite armchair with an ice-cold beer in my hand. Armchair practice allows me the time I need to analyze my entire game

Challenge yourself during practice by putting the ball into one side of the hole, as I'm doing here.

thoroughly and plan what I need to do in order to improve in the future.

You can practice in your armchair after every round. Or, assuming you have an off-season, you should think about what you'd like to accomplish next season and what steps are necessary to reach your goal.

Armchair practice can and should be a lot deeper than you think. It's not just a matter of saying, "Let's see, I played badly today, and the reason is I only hit three greens in regulation. I have to make sure I hit more greens next time." Or "I three-putted five greens—I've got to cut that out." This is simply cataloging what happened, but it doesn't solve anything. You have to determine why you missed the greens, three-putted, or did whatever else it was that hurt your score. Then think about specific steps that will help you change the result in the future.

After each round, you need to consider your errors in execution, but in a more constructive way. You need to know precisely what in your game needs improvement so that you can plan your upcoming practice sessions accordingly.

Sit down and review your scorecard. Start by figuring how many fairways you missed from the tee. How many did you miss to the right? How many to the left? You need to know which side your misses tend to be on, if there's a consistent tendency. If most of the fairways you missed were to the right, did you slice the ball or hit straight pushes to that side? When you missed left, were the shots hooked or were they straight pulls? The prevailing flight of the ball on your tee shots should give you a pretty

I bet you can't guess why armchair practice is my favorite
way of improving my game.

clear picture of what's happening through impact. Say, for example, you missed seven fairways to the right. None of these shots really sliced—instead, they were all pushed or "blocked" to the right, but the ball flew straight. This would tell you that the path of your clubhead through impact was from inside to out (pointing to the right for a right-handed player). Your clubface had to be square to the path the club was moving on—that's why the ball flew straight. From there, you'd know the most important adjustment you need is to get the clubhead moving straight down the target line at impact, instead of from inside to out. You may simply need to move the ball forward in your stance a couple of inches, to give the clubhead more time to reach a square position at impact.

How were your approach irons? Did you miss a lot of greens that were within reach? Analyze your iron swing the same way you did your tee shots. Did you miss greens because you consistently hit the ball "fat," so the ball came up short? If that's the case, you need to consider how level you're staying throughout the swing. A lot of fat shots mean you must be lowering yourself slightly. Imagine yourself holding your position perfectly as your swing revolves around your spine.

If it was a windy day, how well did you cope with it? Did you miss greens with well-hit iron shots because you hit the ball too high and got it caught up in the gusts? Get mentally ready for the next time you're in a strong breeze. Visualize the lower, punched iron shots you'll play by choking up on a longer club, playing the ball a bit farther back in the stance, and keeping your hands ahead of the club-face through impact.

When you missed the green, was it a good miss or a bad miss? By that I mean, did you miss the green on the side where you had a good chance or a slim chance to get the ball up and down? Usually, if the pin is tucked on one side and you miss the green to that side, you won't have much green to work with. If that same side has deep rough or bunkers guarding it, you know you don't want to miss it there. On the other hand, if you miss the green to the far side, you might be farther away from the hole, but with a fairly simple chip to save par. In sum, unless you feel rifle-sharp with your irons, visualize the flight of a solid shot that's shaded a little toward the safe side of the pin.

Think about your day on the greens. You may have putted the ball worse than usual. Maybe you average thirty-two putts per round, but today you took thirty-six. On putts you'd consider makable, did you miss more to one side of the hole or the other? It's possible you didn't line up as accurately as you needed to. Did a lot of your longer putts pull up short today? Maybe you didn't stroke the ball quite as solidly as you can. It's just as important to stroke your putts solidly as it is to make a solid hit with your long clubs. Think about keeping your head really steady next round, and accelerating the putterblade through the ball with your left hand leading.

This is the way you should break down the different physical areas of your game. Always try to determine both your problem areas and sound adjustments that will help you alleviate them in the future.

I AM THE WALRUS

By the way, I don't mean to imply that your arm-chair practice should totally focus on the negatives. You should let yourself savor all the good shots you hit too. Recall your best tee shot of the day and how you felt over the ball and through the swing, including that smooth feeling through impact. Recall, too, the ball's perfect, soaring flight down the middle. Do the same with that nice, crisp middle iron you hit within ten feet of the flag, and that one really good putt you made, a fifteen-footer right in the back of the hole. Remind yourself that these types of high-quality shots are fully within your capability. You simply need to raise the percentage of good shots you hit and lower the percentage of errant ones.

Think also about the mental side of your game. How well did you keep your composure during your round? With my reputation for letting off steam on the course, you're probably wondering, "Who are you, Stadler, to be asking me about my composure?" Well, I still think it's a valid question, even coming from me. Yes, I get angry over bad shots and I show it. However, I'm also the type who expresses my frustration on the spot, then forgets about it and gets on to the remaining business. Believe it or not, I honestly feel that even if I've just scored triple bogey, by the time I get to the next tee I'll be in control of myself and concentrating fully on my next shot. I never let one rotten hole blow me away. Neither should you.

Think back to your own game. Did a bad shot or a bad hole distract you enough so that it led to more bad shots? This is a question only you yourself can answer. From my observation of amateur players, I think a lot of them lose their cool at some point in the round, and when they do, they never get it back. They think too far ahead. They'll say to themselves, "Gosh, I've already made two double bogeys in the first five holes. There's no way I can make it up." Basically, they pack it in for the rest of the round. That's a big reason for crazy fluctuations in amateurs' scores, where a 15-handicapper shoots 81 one day and 93 the next.

I have one last piece of advice. As you have seen, armchair practice can become pretty intensive. So make sure you've got plenty of brews handy before you sink into that easy chair.

3
YOU ASKED FOR IT:

Questions Every Golfer Wants the Answers To

At the time of this writing, I'm in my nineteenth season on the PGA Tour. I've spent a lot of time rubbing elbows with fans at the course and in public places. I also spend a lot of time with amateur golfers playing in the Wednesday pro-ams that precede the regular Tour events. Since these people are helping pay the freight for the tremendous purses we compete for, I always try to be friendly with them and help them out with their games if I can.

Over these nineteen years I've been asked thousands of questions by golfers, regarding how I play certain shots and how they should play them, about strategy, how to get more distance, and so forth. I'm also asked a lot of questions about my experiences on the Tour, about my family and my off-the-course life. Since people always seem interested, I decided to write this chapter to answer these questions every golfer wants the answers to.

This chapter will answer a smorgasbord of questions people ask to help them improve their games (and hopefully yours too). These questions will cover areas such as putting, preshot keys, swing and shot-making situations, short-game play, strategy, and practice. In addition, I'll answer some frequently asked questions about my own game and other dope that Tour players know about. But before we get to the personality section, let's cover some playing questions that might give your game a boost.

You've been one of the Tour's best putters. Can you describe what a good stroke should look and feel like?

To me, the best putting stroke is one that is basically a miniature golf swing. That is, the hands and wrists move the putter naturally back from and through the ball, on the same path that a longer club would sweep through the impact zone.

Many teachers recommend a stroke that is made completely with the arms, with no movement at all in the wrists. The idea is to swing the putter back straight along the target line, while keeping its face square throughout the entire stroke. In theory this sounds good. However, I contend this is an unnatural stroke and therefore more difficult to learn and to maintain.

In what I consider to be the ideal stroke, the hands swing the putter back the same way as on the takeaway for a full shot. That is, the putter naturally swings very slightly inside the target line on the backswing, with its face opening just slightly in relation to the line of putt. On the downswing the putter swings down the target line, with its face perfectly square to the hole. After impact the putter will again swing slightly inside the target line, with its face revolving slightly closed to the target line.

On short putts, this natural rotation of the putterhead will be barely noticeable. However, on long putts this natural rotation becomes easily visible. You can see this happen in my own stroke and in those strokes employed by Gary Koch and Ben Crenshaw—two of the game's all-time best putters.

Of course, in any good stroke there needs to be a nice, even rhythm, with the backstroke and downstroke moving at an identical rate of speed. Any burst of speed, especially at the start of the downstroke, can throw the putter off this natural path.

How do you read the grain in a green? Does grain exist in every green?

To answer your second question first, yes, technically there is grain in virtually every putting green. Grain simply refers to the direction toward which the grass blades are growing on any particular green. As your putt is slowing down and losing momentum, it might turn slightly in the direction the grain is growing.

All greens have some grain, but its influence is more noticeable on Bermuda grass greens than on bent-grass greens. This is because Bermuda grass blades are much more wiry than soft bent grass and might grab the ball more as it's slowing near the hole.

Here are two foolproof ways to figure out the direction of the grain. Study your putt, looking from behind the ball. Does the grass have a shiny look to it? If it does, the grain is running away from you. Therefore, you'll need to stroke the ball a touch softer than normal. If the grass looks dark and dull in color, it means the grain is running against the putt. In this case you must stroke more firmly.

The second way to determine grain is to look straight down at the edges of the cup. You may notice that one side of the cup is clipped clean, while the opposite side looks more ruffled. Remember that the grain is growing toward the side that looks more ruffled.

As far as the exact amount of effect the grain will have on your putts, that's a matter of practice and watching carefully how much the ball reacts to the grain's pull as it slows down. Then it's a matter of adding that calculation to the other factors in your read of the putt.

Is it possible to develop distance control in putting? I three-putt way too often by being long or short on the thirty- to forty-footers.

As with chipping, distance control on long putts must be developed through practice. The more intelligently you practice your long putting, the quicker you'll improve your feel for distance.

Here are some practice recommendations that should help you roll the ball the correct distance.

1. When you practice, don't drop three balls and putt the ball toward the same target. Practice with *one* ball, so you only have one chance to read the putt's speed, not three. This will make you concentrate much harder on each stroke.

2. Alternate the speeds of your longer putts. Putt a forty-footer. Next, hit a thirty-five-foot putt across a side slope; then a forty-five-footer downhill, followed by a fairly flat forty-footer. Don't get overly concerned with your line on these long putts. Always work to make the ball die just as it reaches the hole.

3. Practice long putts under different conditions. Work on all the putts mentioned above just after it's rained, so the green is slow. You probably know what days and times the greens are cut at your home course. It's great to practice long putts right after the greens have been cut, on a dry day, so they're at their fastest. These variations during practice will help you judge speed better on the course.

4. Keep score! During all the above practice, keep score so that your concentration stays sharp throughout the session. You can either putt out on each hole and keep your score against a par of two strokes per hole, or keep count how many times out of eighteen holes you can lag a long one within three feet. With either approach, note your personal best score and always try to beat it.

As you lower your long-putt practice scores, you'll also reduce or eliminate three-putts in actual play.

My friends tell me I have a good-looking, smooth stroke. Yet I hole very few putts. Any guesses why?

Yes. The quality of your stroke is only one third of the total putting equation. The other parts are the quality of your read of the putt, and how well you set up and align the putter to the correct line. You can have the purest stroke in the world, but if your read or your alignment are off, you're almost guaranteed to miss.

Are you getting the read clear in your mind before you step up to the putt? Walk from the hole to your ball to start gathering information. That short walk will give you some feel for whether the putt is uphill or downhill, and to what degree. This is just as important a part of your read as your consideration of the actual line to the hole. Once back to your ball, I recommend you read the line from behind the ball to the hole. This usually gives you the best image of the slope you'll be rolling the ball over.

There are no absolutes in converting the amount of slope into a number of inches of break. Is the putt uphill and the green slow or wet? If so, the putt will break less than you'd think because you'll need to stroke the ball firmly. If you're reading the same amount of slope but the putt's downhill on a fast surface, you'll have to play much more break. This is because the soft putt you'll hit is affected more by gravity. Be alert for grain in the green, how strong it is, and in which direction it's growing. Factor this information into the line you decide on.

Finally, you've got to align your putter very accurately to the line you've determined you must start the ball on. Since it's hard to judge your own alignment, ask a friend to squat down behind you and watch your clubface alignment on some fairly short, flat putts. He or she may give you some feedback that surprises you.

A final suggestion is to use a putter with some

Reading the line from behind the ball will help you determine the subtle break in a green.

type of prominent guide line that's perpendicular to the putterblade (that is, it points down the target line). This will help in getting the ball started where you want to.

What's the best starting point to teach my kids (or my spouse) to get started in golf?

I believe that if you can teach a beginner a proper grip and get them set up to the ball correctly right from the start, the right swing motions and relatively good shots will follow in short order.

Let's work on the grip first. A lot of words have been spent describing the grip, but I think some of them are unnecessary. Also, some significant points get left out. One thing the beginner needs to understand is that the club handle is secured mainly by the fingers rather than the palms. Most beginners will grab the club in a "fisty" grip, like they're holding a baseball bat, unless they're taught otherwise. It's important to let the club rest in the fingers, because this will eventually allow the beginner to fully release the club through the impact zone, helping him or her produce power.

Ask your son, daughter, or spouse to start the grip by resting the club's handle across the palm of the left hand (assuming they'll play "righty"). It will cover the middle section of the index finger and run across the base of the little finger. Next, have him or her close the fingers around the club so that the top of the grip is held securely, but not tightly.

Once the left-hand fingers have secured the club, the beginner closes the left hand naturally over the top of the grip, so that the thumb rests on the top right of the grip. *Note:* If the thumb is either on the top center of the grip, or too far to the right so that the back of the palm is pointing almost straight up, catch this flaw right now. Get that left thumb on the top right of the shaft.

After he or she has completed their left-hand hold, the beginner should be able to look straight down and see the knuckles of the index and middle fingers only. If they see three or four knuckles, adjust the hand more counterclockwise (to the left) on the handle. If they see only one knuckle, adjust their hand more clockwise (to the right) until the second knuckle shows.

The right-hand grip should match the left. By that I mean that if the two palms were open rather than wrapped around the club, they'd be in position to meet each other squarely.

In placing the right hand, ask your beginner to wrap the right little finger around the index finger of the left hand. He or she should close the next three fingers of the hand around the underside of the shaft, then close the palm of the right hand so that it fits snugly over the left thumb. Make sure he or she places the right thumb on the top left of the handle. Many beginners place their right thumb behind the shaft rather than at the top left. It's important they get the right thumb to the left of the center of the shaft. Then the thumb can apply a light pressure so that the grip is secured between it and the palm of the right hand.

Now ask your beginner to place the clubhead on the ground with their grip in place. Both hands should "match"; that is, the palms should be paral-

In assuming the overlap grip, wrap the little finger of your right hand over and around the index finger of your left hand.

lel to each other. In this matching position the line running between the thumb and forefinger of the right hand should be pointing to the inside of the player's right shoulder. If it's not, manually adjust both hands' position until the line points there.

I've described the correct positioning and relationship of the hands to the grip. You hear about "interlocking" and "overlapping" grips, as if the overlapping or interlocking of the hands is the only important factor. It's not. It's the relative positioning of the hands in relation to the handle and to each other that makes for a good grip.

I've advised you to teach your beginner to overlap the right little finger over the index finger of the left hand, as I do. This, obviously, is the overlap grip. An interlock grip simply means the player interlocks the right little finger underneath the left index finger instead of over it. Either method of connecting the hands is okay for the beginner. He or she should go with whichever hold feels more secure.

Now, the setup. The most important point you want to hammer home about the beginner's setup to the ball is that he or she needs to be in perfect balance. Therefore, teach him or her to spread their feet about shoulder-width apart. Also, instruct the beginner to distribute his or her weight as evenly as possible between the feet for all normal shots. Teach the player to flex the knees just a little too.

Next, ask your beginner to hold his or her arms and the club straight out in front of them. He or she should bend slightly from the waist, so the back is straight but angled forward about twenty degrees from perpendicular. Then let the arms relax completely so that the clubhead drops to the ground. Where the club touches the ground is the distance he or she should stand from the ball with that particular club. With a driver, he or she will naturally end up standing farther from the ball than with a nine-iron. But this method of letting the arms relax the club to the ground is a good way of teaching the beginner how far to stand from the ball, which is often a problem area. This method also teaches the beginner to assume a relaxed rather than a tense address posture.

Now that your beginner has a good grip and posture, let's get him or her in the right position relative to the ball. They should position themselves so that the ball is opposite their left heel with the metal-woods, and just ahead of the center of the stance with the iron clubs. Ask them to position their hands to the left of the center of their body, so the hands are even with or just ahead of the ball.

You've given your beginner a lot to learn, so help them assume this grip and setup position regularly in the early going. Also, try to guide them into a square position with their feet, knees, hips, and shoulders all lining up parallel to the target line. However, don't be too fanatical about this at first. The important thing for your beginner is to get the feel of a good grip and a relaxed, balanced setup posture. Once they've mastered this, you can work on getting them square to the target.

How tightly should a player grip the club?

Most higher handicappers hold the club tighter than they need to. This tenses their forearm muscles

A priority for anyone learning the game is to assume a balanced and relaxed setup position.

and leads to a forced, stiff takeaway and back-swing, rather than a smooth, flowing one. Tension also keeps them from coiling as fully as they can.

You'd be pretty surprised at how lightly Tour pros grip the club. You may have seen Fred Couples hit shots where his right hand actually comes off the club after impact. Generally speaking, the pros hold the club very lightly, just enough to support the club through the swing.

The problem is, how do you define the right amount of pressure? I think it varies from golfer to golfer. That's because some players' hands, wrists, and forearms are stronger than others. But I think that relative to each player's individual grip strength, the grip pressure at address should be only a fraction of that player's maximum tightness.

It's been shown that during the swing, your hands and forearms will automatically increase the strength of their hold on the club as needed to support it through all points in the swing. When you're at the halfway point in your downswing, for example, you'll be holding the club much more tightly than you were at address. You don't even have to think about it.

Holding the club with a light pressure at address allows you to make a smooth, slow, full swing of the club away from the ball, which leads to a nice turn, a free downswing, and maximum clubhead speed. There's no need to hold the club in a death grip at address. Just get the swing off to a nice smooth start with a light hold on the club and let your instincts take it from there.

I AM THE WALRUS

Where do you position the ball in your stance? Should this be the same for everybody?

I approach this question a little differently from most teachers. Some instructors say you should position the ball opposite one single position for all shots. Others, and these are probably in the majority, want you to place the ball opposite the left heel with the metalwoods, but move it back with the irons to a point just ahead of the center of the stance.

I actually don't think there are any absolutes to ball placement—only ranges that each individual should know are workable for him or her.

You want to find the lowest point in your swing with the various clubs. With the metalwoods, you should position the ball exactly opposite this lowest point; with your irons, you should play the ball one to two inches back from the lowest point, so you hit the ball with a slightly descending blow. I think this lowest point with the various clubs will be different for each individual. For example, my lowest point is usually a touch farther back in the stance than for other players. I'm definitely on the stocky side; most of my bulk and strength are in my arms, shoulders, and chest. This being the case, my swing is naturally dominated by my upper body. Meanwhile, my legs are a little less active than many other good players'. I don't have as much lateral hip slide toward the target during the downswing as you'll see in some other swing. For that reason, the lowest point in my downswing is usually an inch or two farther back in the stance than it would be for a player with more hip slide toward the target. So I usually lay the ball just behind my left heel with the driver, and at a point midway between my left heel and the center of my stance with the middle and shorter irons. Of course, when playing a specialty shot, such as a low punch with an iron, the ball will be positioned even further back in the stance.

If you're taller and/or more slender than me (and come to think of it, who isn't?), you probably need to generate more power with your lower body. You'll find your lowest point in the downswing might be opposite your left heel or even your left instep with the driver, and opposite or just inside the left heel with your irons. If so, that's where to play it. As in many other areas of the setup and swing, I think every golfer should adjust based on his or her own build.

I'll conclude by saying that you may find the lowest point in your swing varies a little from time to time. You'll occasionally find yourself hitting the ball heavy or thin from your standard ball position. Everybody's chemistry varies a bit from day to day. So don't be afraid to move the ball up or back an inch or two from your standard spot if it helps you solidify your contact.

How high should I tee the ball with the driver?
The best guideline here is to tee up with half of the ball resting above the top of the clubhead. Your goal is to sweep the ball off the tee with the clubhead moving on a level path, or even a touch on the upswing. This gives the shot maximum forward thrust and reduces backspin, so you get maximum distance from the shot.

I AM THE WALRUS

A good driving guideline is to tee up with half of the ball above the top of the clubhead.

By teeing the ball with half of it above the clubhead, you have room to sweep the club through the impact zone without contacting the ground. Keep in mind that the height of the tee will vary slightly depending on the type of club you hit. If it's a deepfaced driver, you'll tee the ball higher than if the driver clubface is shallower, or if you're teeing off with a fairway club.

Why is it so hard for most amateurs to learn an effective golf swing?

First of all, the weekend amateur really doesn't understand how much work goes into developing a professional-level golf swing. They watch tournaments on television, and it looks pretty routine for a player to hit a five-iron 190 yards to within six feet of the flagstick. That's *not* a routine golf shot. If you figure it out mathematically, that shot is within about one percent of perfection. So I believe people's expectations are too high to start with.

That aside, most amateurs don't swing the club effectively because the good golf swing is a full-bodied movement. Most people are used to playing other sports or doing everyday activities while predominantly using their upper bodies. Because of this longtime training, they slash at the ball with their shoulders, arms, and hands rather than incorporating a lower-body turn into the swing. This limits their power, which leads them to swinging harder, which leads to loss of balance and poor contact. Basically it's a vicious cycle.

Higher-handicap players can help themselves a lot by trying to slow down their swings and building a wider swing arc. In building a slower, longer, wider swing motion, they'll be forced to turn their lower bodies on both the backswing and downswing. This will lead to a greater power buildup and more distance with what feels like an easier swing.

Once the player understands this concept, it's still a matter of hitting lots of practice balls with these thoughts in mind. A good golf swing takes time to develop.

Why can't amateurs put backspin on the ball like the pros?

Here are the key reasons amateurs don't spin the ball as well as the pros.

1. Amateurs don't develop as much clubhead speed as the pros. The greater the clubhead speed at impact, the more the ball is "squished" by the clubface. The ball then rolls up the clubface, so that as it leaves the club it's rotating in a clockwise fashion.

2. The golf balls many amateurs play don't spin as much as the pros'. Most amateurs play a ball with a fairly hard Surlyn cover. This cover makes the ball more durable. However, the harder the ball is, the less it grips the clubface, so the less it spins. Take it from me, even the pros would have a hard time spinning the golf balls that the everyday amateur plays with.

3. The amateur doesn't have great lies to hit from. In order to spin the ball, contact between clubface and ball must be clean, with no grass blades getting in between. On the PGA Tour we almost always play off perfect, closely mown fairways where the whole ball is sitting up. Even the best iron players need to compensate for reduced backspin when the ball is down a bit.

I'm convinced amateurs worry too much about backspin. It's not really that big a factor for good scoring. On most courses you, the amateur, won't play to tightly tucked pins like you might see on TV. You'll have some room to let the ball land and run a bit. Just worry about hitting the irons as solidly as you can. You'll find that your most solid iron shots are the ones that stop the best.

Why do I always hit my worst tee shots into the wind, which is when I need my best?

There are a couple of reasons for this problem, which everybody has to some degree. The first is that if you hook or slice a ball into any wind, its sidespin becomes magnified a lot more than you'd realize. What would be a ten-yard fade with no wind can become a thirty-yard slice into a good breeze. Conversely, when you're driving downwind, the sidespin is reduced, so the ball flies straighter than normal.

The second reason, which I think is an even bigger cause, is that most golfers instinctively swing harder when hitting into the wind. This results in poor balance, swaying during the swing, and poor contact.

My advice is when you're playing into a strong wind, resolve to swing easier than you normally would. Three good things usually happen when you do this: 1) You stay in good balance. 2) You make squarer contact. 3) You put less backspin on the ball, which is exactly what you want on an into-the-wind drive. The ball tends to bore through the wind rather than balloon upward, so when it lands you get a little extra roll. (Incidentally, you should always tee the ball the same height with the driver in any wind conditions. It promotes the most consistent contact.)

It takes a lot of discipline to make that smooth, easy swing into the wind, but if you do I think you'll be amazed at the results.

What's your strategy for playing shots in crosswinds, both from the tee and into the green? Should the average amateur take the same approach?

This is an interesting question and a good one because most amateurs don't have a clear plan on what to do in crosswinds.

I AM THE WALRUS

There are two choices. You can start the ball out to the side the wind is blowing from, and let the wind blow the ball back on target. Or you can try to work the ball into the wind so the shot ends up flying basically straight. In other words, if the wind's from the left you draw the ball, and if the wind's from the right you fade it.

I'll use both methods. From the tee, I usually like to ride the wind. That is, if the wind's from the left I'll start it left and let the wind blow it back on target. I may even put a little fade on it, because a fading ball with a left-to-right wind will gain some extra carry. If the wind's from the right, of course, I'll start it out to the right, maybe with a little draw, which again gives it a little extra ride as well as extra roll.

I play this way from the tee because it's the simplest method, the most reliable, and also provides maximum distance. The only time I might try to fight the wind off the tee is on a tight driving hole where I can't start the ball way left or right.

Into the greens, I usually take the opposite approach. If the wind's from the left I'll try to draw the ball, and if it's from the right I'll try to fade it. In both cases I end up with a shot that flies pretty much straight at the target. The reason I do this is that an iron shot that's curving into the crosswind tends to get held up at the top of its flight, so it then drops softly onto the green. It's much easier to hit the ball close to the hole this way. (By the way, remember to take one longer club than normal if you're bending it into the wind.) If you ride the crosswind on your iron shots, the ball won't bite as quickly, so it's tougher to stop it near the hole.

For the average amateur, I'd advise that unless you're very confident in your ability to hit a draw or fade as needed, you're better off aiming to one side or the other as much as the wind demands, and try to hit as straight and solid a shot as you can.

How hard do most Tour pros swing at the ball? Should weekend players do the same?

I can't speak for other players on the Tour, but I can tell you for sure that I never try to hit the ball as hard as I can. On a tee shot on any normal par four, I have the feeling I'm swinging at about 80 to 85 percent of my maximum. With my irons, I swing at about 75 percent of my full effort. The only time I might be tempted to swing harder than 85 percent is on the tee of a par five that's just barely reachable in two. Like most pros, I have a little extra power in reserve when I need it off the tee. But even then I'm still swinging at 90 percent of my maximum.

These percentages are really only my perceptions of what's happening. The truth is that with my 80 or 85 percent swing, I'm hitting the ball about as hard and as well as I can. I'm able to maintain my balance and consistency of clubhead delivery through impact, so every shot is solid. If I tried to hit it as hard as I could, I'd hit one tee shot 310 yards in the fairway, the next 240 in the woods. You can't shoot good scores that way.

Amateurs, if anything, should feel they're swinging even more within themselves than I estimated for myself. You've got to be realistic about how much you play and practice and understand your swing's limitations. The great thing you'll find out is that if you get into the habit of "leaving something in the bag," the end result is you'll hit the ball as far as ever and much straighter too.

What do I do to get the club in the "slot" at the start of the downswing?

This is something I hear golfers ask about all the time. They think of the slot as a precise spot in space that the clubshaft should occupy at some instant after it's started down from the top. It's as if the slot were some position you could have an instructor put you and your club in, have it photographed, then take it home and memorize it so you'd never hit a bad shot again.

Sorry to disillusion you, folks. There's no such thing as a slot, this single miraculous position in space. How can you define it? How far down from the top of the downswing does the slot occur? Does this slot position vary from one golfer to the next?

I'm not trying to confuse you here. All I'm trying to get across is that the term *slot* is a cliché that top players and golf gurus have gotten into the habit of throwing around. When a player is swinging well and making good, solid contact, he or she might refer to getting the club into the slot starting down. What all this boils down to is that the player is swinging the club through the downswing on the correct plane for them, given their height and the distance they stand from the ball.

Now that I've thoroughly disillusioned you, I will say that there's definitely a good way and a bad way to make the transition from backswing to downswing. Start down by smoothly shifting your weight from your right foot onto your left, and turning your left hip to the left, in counterclockwise fashion. If you can accomplish this, your hands and arms will feel like they're simply dropping a bit. This puts your right elbow in close to your side, so as you continue through impact the clubhead will come into the ball moving from inside to along the target line.

Making this lower-body weight transfer while keeping the hands quiet requires discipline. Most people's natural instinct is to overuse their arms and shoulders. I have to remind myself of this often because, as I said earlier, my arms and shoulders are my natural power source. The more slender golfer might find the correct start-of-downswing move a little easier to accomplish than the husky player. But we all have to strive for it. If you can make a correct downswing transition, your chances of swinging the club along the target line through impact are excellent.

Sometimes my iron shots go farther than average from the rough. Why?

Many amateurs don't notice this phenomenon, which happens when you're hitting from light rough. Let's look at an example of what usually happens: You're 160 yards from the hole with a good lie in the fairway. Say that's your five-iron distance. If you hit it solidly, your shot flies on a nice trajectory, lands softly on the green, and comes to a stop not far past where it landed. This shot was hit with good backspin because the club struck the ball a slightly descending blow and no grass intervened between clubface and ball.

Once the downward weight shift action is triggered, the arms, hands, and club automatically drop into the correct on-plane hitting position.

Craig Stadler

Now let's say you've got the same 160 yards—however, your ball has just reached the first cut of rough. The grass is only about two inches long, so you can see most of the ball. You take out your five-iron and make good contact. This time the ball zooms out on a lower trajectory and doesn't peak like the shot from the fairway did. It carries farther, and when it lands it runs like a rabbit. You've hit that five-iron ten to twenty yards longer than normal—usually into trouble.

Remember this: When the ball's sitting pretty well in light rough, always take one club less than you would from the fairway, maybe two less. The pros know this and always take a shorter club from light rough. That's why you hear about these 210-yard six-iron shots in pro tournaments.

Keep in mind that you'll get this flyer effect from light rough only. When the rough is thick and heavy, the opposite effect will happen: the clubhead will be slowed by the heavy grass, so you'll get less distance.

How can I go about improving my shots from downhill lies?

This seems to be a shot nobody likes. I'm not crazy about it myself, to be honest. But with a little understanding of the adjustments that are needed, you can improve your execution of these shots.

When you have a severe downhill lie, your first instinct is to help the ball up, especially when you're playing the shot with a fairly long club. It seems like there's no way you'll get the ball in the air, so you imagine you have to scoop it. This almost always leads to a topped or a fat shot.

I AM THE WALRUS

Here's a key point: Remember that off a steep downhill lie the clubface's loft will be reduced, because when you address the ball you'll be standing pretty much perpendicular to the downslope. So always take a shorter club than normal from a downhill lie. This will solve most of the problem before you even swing.

Once over the ball, position yourself so your shoulders are level with the slope, with your right shoulder higher than your left. Make a compact swing to help your balance, stay as still as possible, and swing the club down along the slope rather than trying to pick the ball cleanly off the grass.

When playing from heavy rough, say five to six inches deep, what's the longest club I should play out with?

There's no one right answer for this. It depends on your individual strength, your swing path into the ball, the type of grass you're playing from, and how deep the ball is sitting.

As a general rule, I recommend weekend players take more loft from deep rough than they think they need to. Here's why: In order to advance the ball effectively from the deep grass, you need to play the ball back in your stance and swing the club on a steep downswing arc. If you try to play the shot as from a normal lie, the clubhead will be muffled in the impact zone by the heavy grass. However, with the ball back in your stance and your hands ahead at address, you'll be delofting whatever club you select. If you try to get out with a six-iron, it'll really have the loft of a four- or five-iron. In most cases, then, this won't be enough loft to get it up and out.

From six-inch rough, I recommend most amateurs use no less loft than an eight-iron. If it's really sitting down deep, play it smart, use your pitching wedge, and get what you can while making sure your next shot's from the fairway.

I'm an 18-handicapper who consistently hits the driver 200 yards. But I can't hit a long iron to save my life. Why? Should I abandon them?

Without seeing this player's swing, it's difficult to say for certain. But from the information given, I'm going to surprise you and say yes, it's likely this type of player should get rid of his or her long irons.

If this player is getting the yardage mentioned while hitting the ball squarely, he or she doesn't generate enough clubhead speed to hit the long irons

On most sand shots, the club should contact the sand about one and a half inches behind the ball.

consistently well. This player will often get much better results with the more lofted metalwoods, even though they actually have about the same loft as the long irons. This is because the lofted metal-woods have shallower clubfaces, so that the mass of the clubhead gets more underneath the ball and thus lifts it into the air better.

I think this player's best set would include a driver with substantial loft, and the four-, five-, and six-woods, with the four-iron being the longest in the bag.

On bunker shots, how far behind the ball should the club enter the sand?

If you're playing from sand of average depth, try to slap the flange of your sand wedge into the sand

To recover from a buried lie in a bunker, the club should contact an area of sand about two and a half inches behind the ball.

one and a half inches behind the ball. If you play from shallow, hard-based sand, it's wise to aim two inches behind the ball to avoid the sole of the club bouncing into it.

When the ball is partially or totally buried, you need to adjust. If most of the ball is below the sand's surface, play the shot with a pitching wedge instead of a sand wedge. This is because the pitching wedge's sharper leading edge will work under the buried ball, whereas the sand wedge might bounce off the sand and "belly" it. Also, because the leading edge must work under the ball, you need to strike the sand farther back, about two and a half inches behind the ball.

How many wedges do most Tour pros carry? Should middle- and high-handicappers do the same?

I would say that the majority of Tour pros regularly carry three wedges. Most of the remainder carry two wedges, the standard pitching wedge and the sand wedge. But there are a few pros who now carry four wedges.

The third wedge most pros carry is an "L" or lofted wedge. This club usually features about sixty degrees of loft, as opposed to about fifty-five degrees for the sand wedge and fifty for the pitching wedge. The L-wedge is great for little flip shots whenever the pin is tucked in close. You can open the blade a little and pop the ball almost straight up so it stops dead when it lands. This club is also good for very short bunker shots.

I think the L-wedge can help out blue-collar golfers, too, but they may not get as much use out of it as the pros do. One reason I say this is that most public courses don't have as much greenside rough as we face on Tour. Also, the greens amateurs play on aren't as fast, so it's not quite as hard to stop the ball. Last, if you decide to carry a third wedge, you have to practice with it and gain a clear picture of when to use it instead of the sand wedge.

There's a big difference between the distances I hit my pitching wedge and my sand wedge with a full swing. What's the reason?

There's usually a wider spread between the lofts on the pitching wedge and the sand wedge than between the other irons. Instead of about three and a half degrees of difference from one iron to the next, there's usually at least five degrees of difference

The less lofted pitching wedge (left) is designed to hit the ball farther than the more lofted sand wedge (right).

here. Pitching wedges usually carry either forty-nine or fifty degrees of loft, while the average sand wedge is about fifty-five degrees. If this is the case with your set, while you might have a ten-yard difference in distance with the numbered irons, the difference will probably be fifteen to seventeen yards between the two wedges.

Another point to keep in mind is that some sand wedges have a lot more than fifty-five degrees of loft. This means the spread is even larger than the one I mentioned, and the distance gap between the wedges is even greater.

Have both your pitching and sand wedge lofts checked on a loft and lie machine. If you want to reduce the spread between them, most clubs can be bent slightly so that loft is added or reduced as needed. You want to make sure there are no big gaps in the distance you get between any clubs in the bag.

When is it okay to use the putter from off the green, as opposed to chipping the ball? Which gives better results?

Many amateurs like to putt the ball from off the fringe. Sometimes it's a good idea. If the ball is just a couple of feet off the putting surface, if the ground is dry and the grass is a little sparse, it makes good sense to putt it. It's a safe shot in that most amateurs control the distance of a putt better than they do a chip.

However, I think some amateurs overuse the putter from off the green. They'll use it out of slightly longer grass and over wet fringe areas, where a rolling ball can easily get caught up and finish well short of the hole.

As a rule of thumb, unless the grass is short and the ground firm, dry, and smooth, go with the chip whenever the ball's more than three or four feet off the putting surface. After all, the chip is really an extended putt. You're simply picking a club that will loft the ball enough to carry it over the fringe and onto the green, so it can roll like a putt the rest of the way to the cup.

What's special about the principles for playing the greenside sand shot?

For a greenside bunker shot, your stance should be open in relation to a line to the hole. That is, for a righty player, your stance and body should point a little left of the hole while the clubface points at the final target.

Because of the exaggerated open stance, you'll automatically make a backswing that's very upright. Coming down into and through the sand, your club will deliver an outside-in, glancing blow, cutting sharply across the ball. This slicing action imparts left-to-right spin on the ball; therefore it will fly high, then drop softly onto the green.

The pros are unbelievably good at the various chip shots. They knock most of them "stiff" and hole out a surprising number. What advice can you give a mediocre chipper?

First, the reason you see the pros chipping it stiff almost every time is that we practice chip shots constantly. I don't think there's a pro on Tour who

When setting up to play a greenside bunker shot, assume an exaggerated open stance (top), since it will allow you to automatically employ the necessary upright backswing (bottom) that's needed for good results.

doesn't put quite a bit of practice time into chipping every week. We're playing at different courses every week, so we know we have to get our touch down pat.

Anyone who's willing and has the time to practice their chipping for about a half hour a day will notice an improved feel for playing this type of shot.

In addition to urging you to practice, I also recommend you get the feel of two clubs that you'll rely on for almost all your chip shots. There's one school of thought that says you should chip with a wide range of clubs depending on how close your ball is to the edge of the green and how distant the cup is. With this method you might be chipping with anything from a five-iron to a sand wedge. I recommend that you use one club for the longer, more running chip shots. This will probably be your six-, seven-, or eight-iron. Your second club, for short chips where you need a little more loft and less roll, will be either your pitching wedge or your sand wedge. (I personally use my sand wedge for almost all my "little" chips.)

If you concentrate your chipping practice on the use of two clubs, it won't take long to develop a great feel for the carry and roll you'll get with each club. You'll start hitting your chips consistently close to the cup and even hole one now and then.

What tips can you give the high-handicapper who's scared to death of hitting the ball over water?

I think weekend players need to combine a realistic understanding of their game with a realistic view of the particular shot at hand.

First, understand the limits of your game before applying it to a given situation. Assess how far you can carry your average tee shot. Let's say you're confident that you can carry a tee shot 180 yards. Whatever your distance with the driver, decide that you'll only try to carry a water hazard if it's *well under* your average driver carry length. If you've got to carry a tee shot 180 yards or more to get over a creek or pond, lay up or play around the hazard.

However, if you need to carry the ball, say, 150 yards over a hazard, it's time to give yourself a pep talk. Instead of thinking, "I've got to get this ball over the water," remind yourself that even with your average hit, you've got plenty of leeway to carry the hazard. Don't think in terms of what will happen if you flub the shot. You'll never improve if you can't overcome this kind of negative thinking. Instead, once you've decided you can definitely carry a water hazard, imagine that it's not even there, and swing away. It won't be long before you get over your phobia.

When you're hitting over water guarding the green, you have even less of a problem. Here you know what club you need to reach the pin. Say it's a six-iron. Usually the pin will be far enough beyond the hazard that you'll feel confident that your average six-iron will carry well over the far side of the hazard. You have an extra option here too. If you think that pin's a little too tight to the hazard for your taste, and there are no major problems at the back of the green, simply take a five-iron, then swing confidently. You may hit it very solidly and knock it into the back fringe. But at the same time you'll be building your confidence in these situations. With time you'll be able to go with whatever iron is best to hit the ball close to the hole.

I'm a fairly powerful hitter, yet I constantly mess up the par fives. These are the holes I should be making up strokes on, not losing more. Any thoughts?

I think many amateurs, particularly the ones who hit the ball fairly long, take the wrong mental approach here. Just because the hole's a par five, they assume it means they have to really bust the tee shot. Consequently, they end up hitting more bad tee shots than usual. If they're not actually in the woods searching for their ball, they're in the rough, from which they'll never be able to get home in two anyway.

Play it smart off the tee. Just try to make a good, balanced swing and make solid contact. Your job's a lot easier if you can play your second shot off the fairway.

Most handicap players, if they're in good shape off the tee, just whale away at their second shots as well. Consider your position and decide: What are the chances of reaching the green in two? If you know you can reach it, great. If you know your best shot can't get there and/or the green is heavily guarded, you should lay up every time. Try to put your second shot in a spot that will leave you an open shot to the pin, at a distance you handle best. If you like to hit a full sand wedge or pitching wedge in the ninety- to one hundred–yard range, position

Craig Stadler

your second shot using the club that will leave you
in that range for your third. This is the way Tour
pros make a lot of birdies on the par-five holes.

Play each shot on a par five with a sound strategy
in mind. You'll find this way you'll score many more
pars and some birdies, while eliminating the sevens
and eights that wreck your round.

*What's the most important club in the bag to practice
with?*

This is an interesting question. The most obvious
answer would be the putter, because you actually hit
the highest number of strokes with that club. Others
might argue that mastery of the sand wedge is para-
mount. But I'm going to say that the most important
club in the bag, and the one you should practice the
most with, is the driver. Why? Because on at least
fourteen of the eighteen holes, it either sets you up
to have a good hole, or it puts you in trouble. If you
think about all the times you've had a disaster hole
that ruined your round, I'll bet almost every one
started with a bad tee shot.

The higher your handicap, the more you need to
practice with the driver. And when I say practice, I
don't just mean beating ball after ball to see how far
you can hit it. What you're after is control of your
swing and solid contact. Work on your setup and
alignment so that you're in good balance and square
to your target. Imagine you're hitting a five-iron instead of a driver, and try to get a flow of smooth
swings going. As I mentioned in Chapter Two, you
should draw an imaginary fairway about thirty-five
yards wide out on the driving range. Challenge

yourself to see how many balls you can put in the fairway for every ten you hit.

If you can put the ball in a nice playable position more consistently from the tee, I guarantee your scoring will improve dramatically.

What's the best way to warm up if you've only got twenty minutes before your tee time?

I realize that most weekend players don't warm up at all before arriving on the first tee, except maybe to hit a few putts. An ideal warmup should take forty or forty-five minutes, but twenty minutes is better than nothing. Here's how to make the most of it.

Start by doing some simple stretching exercises, such as the side bends described in Chapter Two.

Next, hit about a dozen shots in leisurely fashion. That's all you have time for. (If, as a blue-collar player, you're thinking that you're wasting most of a small bucket of balls, get one or two other members of your foursome to split a bucket with you.) Take an easy-to-hit club like a seven-iron and just try to get used to the feel of the ball on the clubface. Don't try to do anything other than swing the club with a nice, smooth tempo. If you want to, hit the last two or three balls with a longer club such as a fairway metalwood. Just getting a little feel for the swing should help you play better on the first few holes.

This whole process, including walking back to the putting green, should take about fifteen minutes. In the remaining five minutes, do the following: Hit four or five basic chip shots with your favorite chipping club; then hit a few medium-long putts (twenty to thirty feet) to get some feedback on the greens' speed. Wrap up your mini warm-up by stroking some two- and three-footers firmly into the cup. You're on your way!

THE "FAN MAIL" SECTION

Many golf fans are eager to learn inside information about Tour players' unusual experiences, habits, personalities, families, and so on. I'd like to share with you answers to some of the questions I'm most commonly asked on Tour.

What is your favorite major championship and why?
To be honest, I don't put as much emphasis on the four majors as some other top players do. Sure, I'd like to win 'em all, but I've never built my year around them the way Jack Nicklaus, Greg Norman, Tom Watson, and some others have.

That said, I'd have to go with the Masters as my number one major of the year. And I'm not saying that because it's the only one I've won. There's just so much that is great about the Masters. It's held at the same site every year, and the fans there really seem to know and love the game. Augusta National is one of the most gorgeous courses in the world and its condition is always impeccable. It also takes kindly to my driving and putting games.

Second on my list is the British Open. I always enjoy playing in Britain. The courses, with their unpredictable bunkers and deep rough, are a change from what we see in the United States. The weird weather we usually encounter there also presents a unique challenge. Generally speaking, I play well in bad weather, and even if it's just cool, it's a nice break to play in cool weather during July. Also, I always get to try out some new ales while I'm over there!

I'd have to rate the U.S. Open third. Sure, I'd love to win it. And it's played on some of the great, historic courses. But my record to date in the Open has been pretty unimpressive. If you look at the record book, the Open is usually won by guys who drive the ball very straight. Curtis Strange, Tom Kite, and Hale Irwin are good examples. I'm not a wild driver, but I'm not the straightest either, and the uniformly narrow fairways of our Open just haven't brought out the best in me. Don't get me wrong—I'd love to pull it off before I hang up the sticks, but I know the odds aren't good.

My least favorite major is the PGA Championship. That's not to say I dislike it or don't hope to win it. However, from my point of view it's not the top event because it's the last major of the year, in August. Usually I'm fresher and more "up" earlier in the year. Also, the PGA seems to be played a lot on courses located where it feels like a blast furnace at that time of year. If anything I'm a better cool weather than hot weather player. I guess I just sweat too much at the PGA in August.

How much do Tour players usually pay their caddies?

Too much! Some caddies make more than a lot of the players! Seriously, most of the regular caddies out here work hard, do a solid job, and deserve what they earn.

Typically, a Tour player will pay his caddie a base salary, which is between $350 and $500 per week, plus five percent of the player's earnings. You can see that the caddie has a big stake in how his boss performs. If the player has a big week and wins, say $60,000, the caddie receives about $3,000 plus his base salary, or about a $3,500 total. If his man misses the cut (and that's true of half the players), the caddie gets his $350 to $500. That doesn't go very far when you're living on the road.

Of course, one out of 150 caddies hits the jackpot every week and packs for the winner. Since most first-place checks are over $200,000 nowadays, the caddie will usually get at least $10,000 himself. That's why they're always jockeying like mad to get the best players' "loops."

Who do you think has the best pure golf swing on the Tour and why?

My vote still goes to Tom Purtzer, who got rolling on the Tour about the same time I did. This is not a terribly original choice, because the players voted him as having the best swing on Tour in one of the major golf publications a few years ago. Tom's swing, in my opinion, still has the finest combination of grace, balance, and tempo that I've ever seen. He also builds a tremendously wide arc and thus generates lots of power.

It's important to note, though, that having the best swing doesn't make you the best player. This is not a knock on Tom, because he's had a lengthy and outstanding career. But a number of players whose swings are far from textbook have won more tournaments and more money. (Me, for example!) Sure, you want to develop the best and most mechanically sound swing you can, but your full swing represents only a fraction of the entire game. You have to work on hitting the ball into the hole as best you can, and that requires a fine short game and putting stroke as well as smart game management.

Do you feel like you've ever had a serious slump?

Truthfully, I don't believe I've ever had a long-term slump. I've had years where I've won tournaments and made a tremendous amount of money, and others that were mediocre by comparison. For example, I was the PGA Tour's leading money winner in 1982 and have finished in the top ten on the money list five times. Yet in 1986 and 1990 I didn't even make the top fifty. These years were part of a seven-year stretch, from the spring of 1984 until the fall of 1991, during which I did not win a PGA Tour event. The press and a lot of fans were really on my case. "When the heck are you gonna win again, Walrus?" I must have heard that a thousand times.

I don't think the golfing public understands what a fine line there is between having a great year and an average one. It can boil down to whether you make or don't make four or five critical shots over the course of the entire year. But those four or five shots are the ones that win you a tournament, maybe two. If those shots don't go your way, you don't win, and then everyone decides you've had a bad year.

During that seven-year winless drought I mentioned, I never won less than $170,000 in official earnings and never placed worse than fifty-third on the money list. True, none of those years could be considered great. But they weren't bad either.

Craig Stadler

Another point about my "long slump" that people don't know is, during that seven-year winless drought on Tour, I won three major foreign events—the 1985 European Masters, the 1987 Dunlop Phoenix in Japan, and the 1990 Scandinavian Open. So I really never went that long between wins, but the U.S. golfing public didn't realize it.

How many holes in one have you made in your life? How many of those have you made while on Tour?

I can't say I remember them all, probably because I celebrated so much at the nineteenth hole. But I believe I've made ten. Interestingly, only two have been since I turned pro. And only one of those two was in actual Tour competition, during a PGA Mixed Team Championship. The other one was during the par-three tournament that's played at Augusta National the day before the Masters starts.

Describe the greatest and the lousiest shots you've ever hit in professional competition.

Believe it or not, I can remember these very vividly, better than I do the holes in one.

The best shot I ever hit in competition came early in my career, at the old World Open in 1978 or 1979. The tournament was played at Pinehurst, North Carolina, on the great *Number Two* course. Anyway, on the thirteenth hole, a par four, I drove the ball into the right rough and pine trees. I had 160 yards to the hole and basically no shot. Well, if you want to call it a shot, I had to hit the ball under some branches, then get up over another tree, and hook it about twenty yards. To top it off, the pin was on the back right of the green and tightly guarded by a bunker. I figured the best I could do was maybe put the ball in the right bunker.

Anyway, I took a medium iron and hit the shot perfectly, a low, rising hook that cleared the various trees, hit just right of the greenside bunker, hopped over the corner onto the right edge of the green, then rolled smack into the cup for an easy eagle. To me that shot beats any hole in one, for sure.

My worst shot as a pro actually came in the final round of a tournament I won. It happened at the 1987 Dunlop Phoenix Open, in Japan. I was playing with Jumbo Ozaki and had a two-shot lead. On the twelfth hole, a long par four, I had 195 yards to the pin from the middle of the fairway. It was a perfect shot for me, just a nice slightly cut four-iron. And I just cold, flat-out shanked the ball. It went about a foot high and seventy yards right, into a waste bunker. I have no clue where that came from because it's the only shot I've shanked in eighteen years on Tour.

Somehow I was able to make believe it didn't happen. I think I scrambled out of the hole with a bogey, and I went on to win the tournament. The lesson in there, I suppose, is to always keep your composure after you shank a shot.

How much do your sons enjoy the game? Do you encourage them to play and compete?

At the time of this writing, my sons, Kevin and Chris, are fourteen and eleven respectively. Chris enjoys all sports and hasn't gotten hooked on golf as yet. Kevin, the older one, has been playing for a number of years now and is coming along very well. He takes lessons from a local professional, and sometimes comes along with me and gets help from Dick Harmon, my coach. At this point he's getting down into the mid-70s pretty consistently, playing from the regular men's tees.

I definitely haven't twisted either of the boys' arms to play the game seriously. If as they get older they find that golf is number one, I'd be pleased and I'd help them all I can, but it's got to be their choice.

The only specific encouragement I've made to Kevin, if you could call it that, was really more of a parental negotiation. Up until about three years ago Kevin played with a cross-handed grip. I really didn't want him to because it's a terrible disadvantage and I suggested he change. But he was stubborn about it.

Then one day he told me he wanted a new set of metalwoods. I said there was only one way I'd get them for him—he had to change to a conventional grip, starting immediately. Now he's implemented the change and is playing very well.

Parenting can be a lot of fun sometimes.

How much time do you take off from the Tour and what do you like to do most when you're away?

I like to play pretty steadily until about mid-October, then get away from competition completely the last two months or so of the year. During this restorative period I concentrate on three things: my family, hunting, and skiing.

As I've mentioned, the Tour is a tough way of life

for a young family. However, I try to spend as much time as I can with my wife and two sons. Many athletes get so involved with their careers that they realize one day their kids are all grown and they can never bring those years back. I'm glad that's not true in my case.

Beyond a variety of recreations with Sue, Kevin, and Chris, I love to hunt and love to ski. We lived in San Diego for about eight years because it was a great environment for the kids. Now that they're older, we've recently moved to Denver. This makes it easy to indulge in my two other passions.

I love skiing. I ski every year even though it's a little risky for a Tour player. So far I've been lucky, though. I did sustain a shoulder injury just before the 1992 season that slowed me down a bit. But even though I don't look pretty lumbering down the slopes, I generally manage to keep myself upright.

I've long since bagged some of the top prizes in hunting and I have mounts at home to prove it. My desert bighorn was downed outside Las Vegas; I bagged a stone sheep on a trip to British Columbia, and a Dall sheep, which is huge, on an expedition to Alaska.

I plan to keep up with my family and hobbies because they're all a lot of fun. But, also, I think getting away at the end of each year has helped me start off each new season with a fresh attitude and has helped extend my career.

What is your favorite club?
My graphite-shafted sand wedge is my favorite club of the fourteen I carry in my bag. That's be-

Craig Stadler

A good sand wedge is a pro's best friend.

cause this very lofted club has helped me to save par when I thought I would score bogey or worse. Not once, but hundreds of times!

I can do so much with my sand wedge—everything from hitting soft, lofted shots from sand or grass to making the ball stop dead from a tight lie in the fairway. My favorite shot is a lob over a bunker to a tight pin.

The light shaft–heavy clubhead combination gives the shaft some whip, or "kick," and thus enhances my feel for playing delicate touch shots around the green.

I AM THE WALRUS

As a kid I practiced wedge shots often. Even to-day, I still enjoy inventing new shots to play with this club. That's the secret to improvised shotmak-ing—staying excited about golf and making practice fun.

To enjoy your practice more and build a strong ar-senal of shots, use a wedge that gives you confi-dence. Also, move the ball around in your stance, experiment with various clubface positions, employ a long and wristy swing, then a firm-wristed short swing, swing extra slowly, then more quickly, and so on.

During your practice sessions, mentally note how the ball reacts in the air and on the ground relative to the changes you made in your setup and swing.

The more shots you learn, the stronger you will be around the greens and the lower scores you will shoot.

What is your most dreaded club?

For some inexplicable reason, I fear facing a three-wood shot out of light rough.

When I think about it, this shot should be hit with more of a sweeping action than a chopping action. So maybe I should move the ball forward slightly in my stance and concentrate harder on making a bet-ter shift of my lower body on the downswing. The trouble is, when you're built like me it's tough to let the lower body lead the downswing. When I reach the top of my swing, my huge upper torso wants to tear at the ball.

I guess I could try trimming down again. But the last time I lost weight, I couldn't hit the ball out of

Craig Stadler

My three-wood is my worst enemy.

my shadow. Besides, I don't want to diet. So I think I'll do the sensible thing to remedy my problem: stay fat and have Spalding ship me a four-wood.

Do you have any nutritional tips for the blue-collar golfer in training?

Don't believe all that stuff you read about eating healthy and needing to be a flat-belly type to swing and play like a pro. I'm living proof that being your-self and eating what makes you feel contented is the way to go.

When I have a full stomach I think more clearly and swing better too.

At home, I like to start the day with some good

I AM THE WALRUS

You wouldn't leave for a hunting trip without putting gas in your pickup. So don't play golf on an empty stomach. Fill it up!

old-fashioned bacon, eggs, home fries, toast, juice, and coffee.

For lunch, I enjoy biting into a few chili dogs and sipping a couple of ice-cold beers.

For dinner, if it's too late for my wife, Sue, to prepare something American, I enjoy swallowing down some beef tacos with some more ice-cold beer.

For dessert, the standard ice cream sundae and chocolate cake are still favorites of mine.

In the evening, potato chips and onion dip make watching television a pleasure.

On the road, when I'm usually on the go at a particular country club, I grab what I can during the day: something like burgers, baked beans, and fries.

In the evening, I'll go to one of my favorite on-the-road hangouts, and sort of close my eyes and point to something on the menu. However, on those rare occasions when I'm in the mood to sit in a high-class restaurant with a client, I'll order venison or wild boar, or some kind of exotic game bird with all the trimmings. Later, I'll smile when the man or woman sitting across from me says, "Check, please."

THE WALRUS'S TRAVEL GUIDE:

My Favorite Tournament Courses and Night-Spot Restaurants

When I'm on the run, I don't run to just any restaurant.

Tournament	Course(s)	Restaurant(s)
Pebble Beach Pro-Am (Pebble Beach, CA)	Pebble Beach Spyglass Hill Poppy Hills	Hog's Breath Forge in the Forest
Los Angeles Open (Palisades, CA)	Riviera	Rex's Fish Market Tony Roma's
Bob Hope Classic (La Quinta, CA)	Indian Wells PGA West Bermuda Dunes La Quinta	The Nest Wally's Desert Turtle Las Casuelas Nuevas Marie Callendar
Buick Invitational (San Diego, CA)	Torrey Pines	Dini's Hawk and Dove
The Player's Championship (Ponte Vedra, FL)	TPC at Sawgrass (Stadium)	Sawgrass Beach Club Homestead Ragtime
The Masters (Augusta, GA)	Augusta National	Green Jacket
Heritage Classic (Hilton Head Island, SC)	Sea Pines	CQ's Hudson's

I AM THE WALRUS

Tournament	Course(s)	Restaurant(s)
Byron Nelson (Irving, TX)	TPC at Las Colinas	Four Seasons Bennigan's
Memorial Tournament (Dublin, OH)	Muirfield Village	Friday's
World Series of Golf (Akron, OH)	Firestone	Diamond Grill Nick Anthe's
Walt Disney World Classic (Lake Buena Vista, FL)	Magnolia Palm Buena Vista	Enzo's Pizzeria Lee and Rick's Chatham's Place The Mill

4
THE RULES RULE:

It Pays to Play by the Book

To most weekend golfers, learning the rules of golf backward and forward is a pain in the rear. Let's face it, nobody really wants to spend their time studying the *USGA Rules of Golf* when they could be playing the game or otherwise enjoying themselves. But one of the most appealing features of the game of golf is that it's basically played on the honor system. Players at all levels are expected to police themselves. And on the PGA Tour, for the most part, we do that pretty darn well. I can't think of any incidents in my career where a player consciously decided to gain an advantage by breaking a rule—disagreements about a certain rule or situation occur, certainly; consciously breaking a rule in a PGA Tour event, no.

I'd like to think the reason PGA Tour players always go by the book is that as a group, we're the most honorable athletes in sport. But I'm sure there's another reason too. There's way too much to lose out here to risk being caught cheating. It's not just a matter of a player being disqualified from a particular event; he'd probably be suspended from the Tour for an indefinite period. Definitely not worth the risk!

I get a kick out of watching other sports and seeing what players get away with, though. I believe the "zebras" could call holding on just about every play in an NFL football game. A blocker practically has to pull a tackler down by the face mask before anything's called. Basketball is almost as bad with all the wrestling matches under the hoop. If I played golf the way these other guys compete at their games, I'd be teeing the ball up in rough, kicking the ball down the fairway, and using a scoring pencil with an eraser.

I wish all you amateur players would follow the example set by PGA pros and adopt a stricter standard of fair play for your weekend matches. My reason is that you are part of the golf population of twenty-five million, whose unwritten responsibility is to uphold the dignity of the game. Realize, too, that the rules are designed to help you, not hurt you. Also, if you become known as a guy who plays it straight no matter what, your opponents will probably be less likely to try to pull anything when they're playing with you.

MY BRUSH WITH THE LAW

If you've followed golf for a while, you might be saying, "Wait a minute, Stadler. Aren't you the guy who got thrown out of a tournament a while back for some kind of hanky-panky?"

Well, to give you the short answer to this, yes. I was disqualified from the 1987 San Diego Open. Now that I've admitted that, you owe it to me to let me explain exactly what happened.

This rules gaffe took place on the fourteenth hole of the third round of the tournament, although I didn't find out about it until right after I'd finished the fourth and final round. I'd played quite well that week and a second-place finish appeared to be locked up.

Anyway, on the fourteenth, I pushed my drive right. The ball came to rest under the limbs of a small pine tree. It was under the limbs on the fairway side of the tree trunk; so being right-handed, it would be possible for me to advance the ball. However, the lowest limbs on the tree were about two and a half feet off the ground, so I couldn't take a normal stance and swing the club. I could hit it, however, by ducking under the branches and playing the shot from my knees. I decided to give this a try rather than "wimp out" and take a penalty stroke for an unplayable lie. I just wanted to advance the ball as far as I could toward the green.

Next, I picked out an iron and started to get in position to play the shot. That's when I realized that I'd mess up my light-blue slacks if I knelt down on the grassless ground beneath the tree. (Yeah, I know, I'm supposed to be the kind of guy who doesn't notice if his shirttail is out and his shirt isn't buttoned. But the tournament was being televised, and I didn't want to finish a round on national TV looking like a gardener.)

Craig Stadler

So I made my fatal mistake. I placed my golf towel on the ground beside the tree. Then I knelt on the towel and hit the ball out. Everything seemed normal. I went on to finish the tournament apparently in second place and felt it was a great week.

However, there was a fly in the ointment—caused, ironically, by the damned television, which had been the reason I hadn't wanted to get my pants dirty in the first place. It seems that a golf (and rules) enthusiast from Iowa had phoned in to the PGA's tournament headquarters and reported that I'd placed a towel on the ground and played my shot from it. Was that possibly a violation of the rules? (By the way, I never did find out who you were, but thanks again.)

Well, you might be saying, I can guess the rest. You took a penalty for some type of rules breach and it cost you some bucks, right?

Unfortunately, wrong. A PGA Tour official, Glen Tait, approached me and asked whether I'd kneeled on a towel while playing the shot. I said yes. Next he informed me that by doing so, I was guilty of *building a stance*—that is, of playing a shot from a stance that had been unnaturally improved. (I wish I'd had the presence of mind to tell him I hadn't even taken a stance, that I'd been kneeling.) Since this was in violation of the rules, I would have to take a two-stroke penalty. Now for the kicker: Because my scorecard had already been signed and had been posted without counting the penalty, which had been determined after the fact, I'd turned in a score two strokes lower than the final result. Therefore, I was disqualified from the tournament.

So it was good-bye, San Diego Open, and good-bye, second-place finish.

You might expect that I'd respond like a raving lunatic at this harsh application of the rules. (I'll always think it was unjust, because I *know* that I had no intention of taking some advantage by laying down that towel, nor did it give me any actual advantage.) But I'm proud to say I didn't. When everything finally sank in, I said to myself, "The hell with it. I'm getting a bad deal, but I'll live."

Now, I will admit that some longer-reaching effects of my disqualification really did tick me off when I found out about them a couple of weeks later. You see, according to PGA Tour rules, because I'd been disqualified from a tournament, I couldn't contend for that year's Vardon Trophy, which goes to the player with the lowest stroke average. I'd never won the Vardon Trophy, although I'd been close a couple of times. It was an achievement I'd always hoped to accomplish. And I'd had a terrific start in 1987; I'd shot 62 twice on the early West Coast swing, which was the best score shot on Tour up to that point. If I hadn't been booted out of the Vardon Trophy standings eight weeks into the season, I'm sure I would have at least been a contender.

Another thing: I was disqualified from the rankings of the Tour leaders in the various statistical categories we have, such as driving distance, greens in regulation, subpar holes, and sand saves. There's some recognition from your peers and the fans for leading a category, not to mention a $25,000 bonus for doing so. At the time of the final ruling, a couple of weeks after San Diego, I led the tour in subpar holes, and was third in putting and fifth in driving distance. It's fair to say I'd have had a pretty good shot at leading at least one category for the year. And I really thought that because of the bizarre circumstances of the "towel penalty" and the subsequent disqualification at San Diego, I'd receive a little consideration regarding these other slights just mentioned. No such luck.

The morals of this rules fable are as follows:

1. Become more familiar with the rules. At the very least, study them during the upcoming off-season, if you refuse to learn them right now.

2. Whenever you're in some type of course situation where you're not completely sure of a particular rule, ask your playing partner about the options.

It pays to play by the book.

3. *Never kneel on a towel while playing a shot—especially not when you're on TV.*

THE BLUE-COLLAR GOLFER'S TWENTY MOST COMMON RULE AND ETIQUETTE VIOLATIONS

I probably play at least fifty rounds a year with amateurs, either in the Wednesday pro-ams or in casual rounds at home. And I've got to say that, as opposed to the PGA Tour, I see an awful lot of rule violations by weekend players.

A greater number of amateurs, in my opinion, violate the rules because they don't have a clear understanding of them. Maybe when they took up the game, they observed that other golfers were handling situations like lost balls or unplayable lies a certain way, and the new player assumed that what he or she saw was the "right way." Or, quite often, when a player is in a regular foursome, everybody pretty much agrees on some basic rule bending, as long as everybody does it the same way. Well, all I've got to say is, if you ever start entering organized competition, you may find out that your previous cozy interpretations of the rules can get you in trouble.

That said, I'd like to present you with the blue-collar golfer's twenty most observed rule (and etiquette) violations. I'll try to describe them in the basic order they might occur during play of a hole, first mentioning breaches that occur at the teeing area, then those that usually occur between tee and green, and finally those that take place on the green. If you frequently violate any of them, there's no time like the present to stop and learn the "right move" guidelines I've provided.

Violation #1: *Carrying Too Many Clubs.* Just a reminder to those of you who don't know: you're limited to carrying a total of fourteen clubs. I point this out because I realize that with all the club manufacturers vying for your business, you're bombarded with advertisements for new clubs, all designed to help you shave strokes off your score. Many amateurs, particularly you real golf nuts, add some new clubs all the time. My question is, when you add a club to your bag, do you ever take anything out?

Nowadays, for example, many manufacturers are praising the merits of highly lofted metalwoods that you can hit out of almost any lie. Over the years many golfers might have added a five-wood, then a six- or seven-wood; then maybe even a nine-wood. On the short end of the set, instead of having just two wedges, three- and even four-wedge systems are quite common. I just want to remind you that if you happen to be carrying six metalwoods and four wedges in your bag, you'd better be carrying only three iron clubs (plus the putter). I think you're probably "overclubbed."

The Penalty: In match play, you'd lose the hole you played while carrying fifteen or more clubs. The maximum deduction per round is two holes. Take it from me, it's really tough to come back if, on the sixteenth tee, your opponent spots a fifteenth club in your bag and you're already one down. In stroke play, you'd be penalized two strokes if the infraction was discovered before you teed off on the second hole. If it happens after teeing off on the second hole or beyond, you'll be penalized four strokes. This happened to Johnny Miller in the first round of the World Series of Golf some years ago. Miller found that his son's junior-size putter was stuck down in the bottom of his bag. He didn't even know it, much less consider playing with a club about two feet long. Well, as Johnny can tell you, those four-stroke penalties are hard to make up.

The Right Move: Whenever you decide to try out a new club, take another club out on the spot. If you want to try out an extra wedge, decide which longer club to do without. Or, if you just picked up a new metalwood, decide which iron club you won't need too much. And take it out at your car or locker, not when you're on the first tee.

Violation #2: *Teeing Up Ahead of the Markers.* I'll bet Sigmund Freud or some current pop psychologist would have fun with this one. How many times have you seen someone put their tee peg in the ground just inches *ahead* of the tee markers? A lot more often than you'd expect. Maybe you do it yourself. It may be a subconscious need on the golfer's part to gain some small edge in playing the hole. Or maybe he or she just doesn't understand that the teeing area is actually an imaginary rectangle. This rectangle extends back two club lengths from a line drawn between the outside limits of the markers themselves. The ball must be teed between the front and back lines of this imaginary rectangle, as well as between the perpendicular lines connecting them.

The Penalty: No loss of hole involved in match play. However, your opponent can require you to replay another ball from within the teeing area. In stroke play, this breach will cost you two strokes, plus you must then play another ball from within the markers.

The Right Move: Know the margins of the teeing ground. Remember that the ball must always be between the markers, never ahead of them, and never more than two club lengths behind them (which is about seven feet).

Also, keep in mind that using the entire teeing area, including setting the ball back a bit from the front edge, can be a nice advantage to the smart player. You may be able to find a more level lie for your tee shot a bit back from the markers—an edge that's definitely worth a few feet. Or, say you're on a par three and your distance is precisely between two clubs. You can take the stronger club, then tee the ball near the back border of the teeing area. If you hit the shot you planned, it'll finish closer to the hole.

Violation #3: *Asking Your Opponent What Club He or She Hit.* Say the golfer is playing a par three on a course he or she has never seen. It's windy. The opponent, who plays there regularly and hits the ball about the same length as the visitor, hits a well-struck shot onto the green. The visiting golfer says, "Nice shot. What club was that?"

The Penalty: As soon as those words are out of the player's mouth, his or her opponent can call a penalty. In match play it's loss of hole. In medal play it's two strokes.

Remember, there's no rule against *looking* to see what your opponent hit. Also, in match play, it's okay to discuss club selection with your partner or your caddie.

The Right Move: Obviously, don't ever ask an opponent what club he or she hit. But I recommend something else: Don't even try to "hawk" the other player's bag to determine what club was used. Why? Because you don't know what they were trying to do with any particular shot. They may have swung a little harder or softer than normal. They may be hitting the ball extra solidly that day. My point is to know your own game and learn to rely on your own judgment. You'll be a better player for it.

Violation #4: *Playing an Out-of-Bounds Ball from Somewhere Near Where the Ball Left the Course.* This one happens all the time. It usually goes like this. The player hits a big hook or slice that looks like it's going out of bounds. But nobody can say for sure that it's out. At any rate, the golfer hurries to where he or she hopes to find the ball in bounds, but has no luck.

So the player usually does one of the following wrong things.

1. Drops a ball near where the original went out, and takes no penalty.

2. Tosses another ball onto the fairway as above, and takes a one-stroke penalty so he or she is now lying two.

3. Plays a second ball from the tee, and assumes he or she lies two after this shot.

4. Drops another ball near the out-of-bounds markers, as close as possible to where the ball was likely to have gone out, and takes a one-stroke penalty.

5. Tosses another ball onto the fairway, roughly parallel to where the ball went out, and takes a two-stroke penalty, so that he or she is now lying three.

The Penalty: Whenever a ball is hit out of bounds, the penalty is *stroke and distance.* This means that the player must count the first stroke played, add a one-stroke penalty, and then hit again from the original position. If the player has hit the tee shot out of bounds, for example, he or she would play a second ball, after which he or she would be lying three.

The Right Move: Whenever you've hit a ball you think might be out of bounds, play a "provisional ball." Don't rationalize that you'll find the ball in play, so you can then reason that you don't need to hit another ball. Because once you find out the ball is "OB," the next rationalization takes place. That's when you say you don't want to go all the way back to the original spot. That reasoning would then lead you to choose from items 1 through 5 (depending on just how far you want to go in breaking the rules).

By playing a provisional ball, you're covered. If your first ball's in play, great. If not, your provisional is also out there, so you're ready to take your medicine and go on.

I AM THE WALRUS

Violation #5: *Searching for a Lost Ball for an Indiscriminate Amount of Time.* A player hits one into the "boonies," and goes out and starts looking for it. And looking. And looking. You don't really want to point out that your hair is turning gray in the meanwhile, but you finally tell the player you're afraid the ball is lost. Grumbling, Mr. Lost Ball drops one in the fairway and plays out the hole with a one-stroke penalty.

The Penalty: A player has *five minutes* to search for a lost ball from the moment he or she arrives at the area the ball has landed in. Then, if the player did not hit a provisional from the tee, he or she must go back, play a second ball, and take a stroke-and-distance penalty. (When you tell the player this, it might tick him off, but you're in the right. By the way, while Mr. Lost Ball is storming back to the tee with smoke blowing out of his nose, make another smart move and wave the group behind you through. After all, how many minutes have they been standing there waiting?)

The Right Move: I know that golf balls are fairly expensive and you hate to lose them. Still, realize you're going to lose a ball every now and then. That's part of the cost of playing the game. That said, try to be realistic about the time you spend looking for a lost ball. I'm not asking you to use a stopwatch. Just be aware. Ask a playing partner, "Have I used up my five minutes yet?" Also, if you've hit a shot well off target and deep into the woods, maybe you're better off realizing it rather than wasting even five minutes.

Craig Stadler

Last, hit that second ball so you don't have to hike back to the tee.

Violation #6: *Taking an Improper Unplayable Lie.* In this situation, a player's ball has finished close to a bush, a tree, or in some other position from which it can't be advanced. The player moves the ball as far as necessary to clear the impediment and drops the ball, taking a one-stroke penalty.

The Penalty: It's correct that the player will incur a one-stroke penalty when the ball is declared unplayable. However, taking the one-stroke penalty does not allow the player to move the ball as far as necessary to be clear of the impediment. The ball may be moved only two club lengths. By moving it an indiscriminate distance, he or she would lose the hole in match play, or be penalized two additional strokes in stroke play.

The Right Move: A player actually has three options when declaring a ball unplayable, as follows:

1. Take a one-stroke penalty and move the ball no more than two club lengths to either side of the ball's position, making sure that the ball is not moved closer to the hole. (This is probably the most-used option as well as the most preferable one.)

2. Sometimes the ball's location is such that moving it two club lengths to either side will still not allow you to play it. If so, you can move the ball as far back from its original position as needed to have a shot. Just make sure to keep the ball's original position between you and the hole.

3. If you are unable to play the ball by taking either of the above steps, which is rare, you must go back to where the original stroke was played and hit another ball from there, adding a stroke-and-distance penalty just as for a lost or out-of-bounds ball.

Violation #7: *Incorrect Placement of the Ball After Hitting It into a Lateral Water Hazard.* Suppose the golfer is playing a hole with a water hazard along the right side. He or she slices the ball into the hazard. The player then estimates the position at which the ball landed in the hazard, drops a ball approximately parallel to that position on dry ground, and takes a one-stroke penalty.

The Penalty: When you hit your ball into a lateral water hazard, you have to take a one-stroke penalty. However, you must drop the ball within two club lengths of the position at which the ball last crossed the boundary of the hazard.

The Right Move: You can't just guess where the ball landed in the hazard and move it out laterally as described previously. Follow the correct procedure. After swinging, mark the spot where the ball last crossed the hazard. Walk directly to that spot without taking your eyes off it. Then drop a ball within two club lengths of that point.

Violation #8: *Incorrectly Dropping the Ball Away from Casual Water.* A player is entitled to free relief whenever the ball comes to rest in a puddle or any area of standing water. But suppose the player's ball has come to rest in a puddle in the rough, close to some trees. The player announces he or she is taking a drop from casual water, then drops the ball on the fairway. The player has moved the ball farther from its original position to get to the fairway, rather than dropping at the point of nearest relief on dry ground.

The Penalty: If this violation were not rectified, the penalty would be loss of hole in match play, two strokes in stroke play.

The Right Move: When your ball comes to rest in casual water, first determine the shortest distance from your ball to the edge of the casual water area. (This is a point at which you can no longer draw up water while fairly taking your stance.) Once you've determined this shortest distance from your ball to the end of the casual water, you're allowed to drop the ball one club length, no closer to the hole, from that point. You can't simply decide where you want to drop the ball—even if dropping it at the nearest point of relief from the casual water puts you closer to the trees so that you're blocked out.

Violation #9: *Pressing Down on the Ground Immediately Behind the Ball.* This is a violation I think some golfers commit unconsciously. That is, they actually don't realize they're pressing down on the ground either with their foot or the clubhead. But they are. The effect is that the lie of the ball is improved—there won't be anything immediately behind the ball to either snag the club on the takeaway or get caught between clubhead and ball at impact.

The Penalty: Loss of hole in match play; two-stroke penalty in stroke play.

The Right Move: Do nothing! Be consciously aware that you can't press down any ground in the immediate vicinity of the ball without it being considered improving the lie.

If you realize you've been doing this, I have a suggestion that will help. Whenever you practice, hit your shots out of imperfect lies. When you fish a ball out of the practice pile, just roll the ball over to a spot and hit it from there. Don't fiddle the ball into a perfect, perched-up lie so it's just begging to be hit. After all, what are the odds of the ball coming to rest like that out on the course?

Once you get into the habit of practicing from average lies, they won't look so bad in actual play that there's any temptation to improve them.

Violation #10: *Removing Impediments That Are Not Loose from Around the Ball.* Lots of times, a player's ball will come to rest amongst some loose impediments. These are items that, as their name implies, are not fixed or growing but rather are just lying there. They include sticks, twigs, cut grass, dead leaves, loose stones, and the like. The golfer may pick up or brush away any loose impediments from around the ball.

However, it's a violation to pull away any items that are fixed or growing from around the ball. Specifically, you can't pull out any grass, weeds, or brush that's lying around or behind the ball.

A pretty famous example of an alleged breach (although it could not be proven) actually occurred during one of the early Skins games between Tom Watson, Gary Player, Jack Nicklaus, and Arnold Palmer. As it happened, Gary Player's ball was slightly off the green, and Gary started doing some "housecleaning" that Watson didn't take kindly to. After the round Watson accosted Player in the parking lot and accused him of breaking the "loose impediments" rule. No action was taken, but it caused quite a bit of tension.

The Penalty: If you're caught removing fixed impediments from around your ball, the penalty is loss of hole in match play, two strokes in stroke play.

The Right Move: Don't try to get away with anything such as removing a few loose impediments from near your ball while at the same time picking some live grass from around your ball. Sure, you'll probably get away with it. But really, is it worth it? Picking out a couple of strands of grass is of almost no physical benefit to your next shot. Of course, if you're pulling it out by the handful it will help, but then you're going to get caught and look really stupid as well. If it's fixed and growing, just stop right there.

Violation #11: *Playing a Moving Ball.* Occasionally you'll find your ball has come to rest in a not-quite-stable position outside a hazard. Let's say, for example, the ball is propped up high on fairway grass or lying atop loose material in the rough, such as pine needles.

The player assesses his or her shot, then steps into the address position, waggling the club and eyeing the target. At some point while the player is addressing the ball with the club grounded behind it, or just as the backswing starts, the ball moves. Usually in these cases the ball's movement is very slight, almost imperceptible. It's possible, even likely, that no one else in the group could spot the movement. But you, the player, did.

The Penalty: In either stroke play or match play, if the player's ball moves at any time during the address or during the swing prior to contact, it's one stroke.

The Right Move: Sorry, friends, but this is one of those times where the rule book isn't too friendly. If the ball moves on you at all, own up to it and call yourself for the one-stroke penalty. Remember that you've only incurred a penalty if the ball changes its position at address or during the stroke. It's okay if the ball just jiggles a tiny bit, as long as it jiggles and returns to its original position. More than likely you'll be the only player able to detect this and the only one who can make the call.

I know, I know. You're going to say that even if the ball did move you didn't really move it yourself and you weren't trying to gain an advantage, so why do you have to take a penalty? Well, this is a case where, I'll agree, the rule book is just plain rigid. It ticks me off too. But understand the reason for this black-or-white interpretation. If players were allowed to say, "It only moved a little, I shouldn't be penalized," well then, how much does a ball have to move before a player is penalized? It'd be a never-resolved argument. Since the rules are there to make certain that competition is always as fair as possible to all concerned, any ball that moves is subject to a penalty of one stroke.

Violation #12: *"Rearranging" Branches That Impede Your Stance or Swing.* It's a common occurrence to knock a shot off line, close to some trees with relatively low-lying branches (as in "My Brush with the Law" earlier in this chapter). The player may find that either the stance or some part of the swing will be blocked by branches. If these branches are relatively flexible, you'll sometimes see a player actually arrange them into a sort of intertwined package so that they no longer block the stance or swing. Or at least it makes the shot much more playable. (Actually, some of the more flagrant rule abusers aren't even this tactful. They'll *break* the branches off if they can.)

The Penalty: Whenever a player physically changes the position of fixed and growing plants that in any way improves the play of the shot, he or she is subject to a two-stroke "hit" in stroke play. It's loss of the hole in match play.

The Right Move: Say your ball comes to rest close to a tree or bush that will be behind you as you make the stroke, so it limits your stance and/or backswing. You *are* allowed to fairly attempt to assume your stance over the ball. If this means your back pushes against some flexible branches that are directly behind you, that's okay. And, in the act of hitting the shot, if your arms or the club contact the branches and move them, there's no penalty either.

Violation #13: *Grounding Your Club in a Hazard.* Technically, there are only two types of "hazards" on a golf course—any form of water hazard, and sand traps or bunkers. Rough and trees are not technically hazards, although they do affect your play of the shot.

Of the two official hazards, golfers are likely to try to play the ball from sand a lot more often than from water, although they'll occasionally try to extract a ball at the edge of a water hazard. In either, the player grounds the sole of the club behind the ball as he or she would from other positions on the course. Or the sole of the club touches the surface of the hazard as the clubhead is swung back.

The Penalty: If you ground your club within a hazard while your ball is in the hazard, the penalty is two strokes in stroke play, or loss of hole in match play.

The Right Move: Obviously, it's to understand this rule and make sure that you hover the clubhead slightly above the sand or water at all times. I think almost all amateurs who ground the club in a hazard do so out of ignorance, rather than in an attempt to make their shot easier. That's the reason for the rule, incidentally—if your clubhead is grounded in the sand, then you draw it back, you've actually improved your lie because you've moved some sand out from behind the ball.

One other suggestion that will help in those rare instances when you're getting set to play from the edge of a water hazard: *Don't take any practice swings from within the hazard.* If your club contacts any surface within the hazard, it's loss of hole or a two stroke penalty. A few years ago in a televised Tour event, Andrew Magee's second shot missed the green left, kicked down an embankment, and came to rest in a mushy patch near the edge of a lake. In prepping to play the shot, Magee took some practice swings next to his ball. A Tour official immediately came up and assessed him two penalty strokes because his club contacted the ground. His ball was resting just inside the red line marking the boundary of the hazard! (So you see, I'm not the only guy on Tour who's felt like a jerk because of unwittingly violating the rules.)

Violation #14: *Placing an Extra Club in a Sand Trap While Playing the Shot with Another One.* Suppose a player hits his or her tee shot into a fairway bunker on a par-four or par-five hole. Often the player won't know for sure what club to use until he or she has inspected the lie and judged how much loft is needed to clear the lip. That being the case, the player takes two or three clubs, walks into the trap, decides what club to use, then pushes the other club or two into the sand, but still inside the hazard.

The Penalty: Here the player can be tagged with the same penalty as in #13—two strokes in stroke play or loss of hole in match play. The reason is, in pushing the club(s) down into the sand, the player can rightfully be accused of testing its texture.

The Right Move: Personally, I think this is a pretty picky interpretation of the grounding-in-a-hazard rule. It can be levied against you, though. Technically, an opponent can claim that by placing another club down inside the hazard, you've gained information about the texture of the sand that will help you in playing the shot. (By the way, I've never seen an extra club placed in a water hazard—only thrown in! And I've never seen a penalty called for doing that.)

The right move is simple—always walk into a sand trap with only one club in your hand. In a situation where you're not sure what club you might need, take three clubs out of the bag—the one you think you're most likely to use, along with the next stronger and next weaker club. Assess the shot from behind or to one side of the bunker, pick up the club that you think is best, then enter the trap. On the rare occurrences when you begin to set up to the ball and find out you need another stick, step out of the trap and grab it.

Violation #15: *Dropping the Ball Outside a Water-filled Trap.* You may be one of those diehards who'll play golf any time the course is open. Since this definitely includes playing in wet weather, you should be aware of this violation.

On a par-four hole, a golfer hits his or her second shot into a greenside bunker. Because of heavy overnight rain, the bunker is filled with water. The player fishes the ball out and drops it behind the bunker, no closer to the hole. He or she then pitches onto the green, takes one putt, and tells the opponent to mark down a four. The opponent says, "That was a five."

The Penalty: A ball that has finished in a hazard must be played from within that hazard for no penalty to occur. If the ball must be dropped out of a hazard, the player takes a one-stroke penalty for removing the ball (in match or stroke play).

The Right Move: There are two possible options:

1. You must drop out of the hazard, no closer to the hole, and add a stroke. Be sure to keep the ball's original position between you and the hole.

2. You can also play the ball as it lies, with no penalty. Actually, this isn't a bad idea if part of the ball's surface is above the water (and you've got a good pair of waterproof shoes). You can play it almost as if it's a regular bunker shot. Just remember to pull down hard on the downswing and make the leading edge of the clubface contact the water a little farther behind the ball than you would if you were contacting sand.

Violation #16: *Tapping Down Spike Marks on Your Line of Putt.* The player notices several spots close to the hole where blades of grass have been kicked up by the spikes of earlier players. The golfer realizes these grass blades can deflect the roll of the ball, especially since it will be losing its speed as it approaches the cup. So he or she taps these spike marks down with the sole of the putter.

Now that all of the repair work has been done, the player can go ahead and make the stroke, confident that the ball will not be thrown off its line. Sounds fine, doesn't it? Wrong!

The Penalty. Under the rules, players are not allowed to tap down spike marks anywhere on their line of putt prior to holing out.

There's been a great deal of discussion over the years whether spike mark repair should be allowed. The reasoning is that spike marks can be an impairment to the line of putt just like ball marks, which may be repaired, so why can't spike marks be fixed too? The USGA (and the PGA Tour) have not bent on the spike mark question, though. I guess their reasoning is that if everyone could repair spike marks, they'd spend all day "gardening" their line of putt, and the game would get even slower than it is. (I definitely have to agree on that point. In case you haven't noticed, I'm one of the fastest players on the Tour. I hate to take five hours to play a round.)

Also, there really is a difference between ball marks and spike marks in that ball marks can't be helped. When a high-flying iron shot hits a receptive green, it will leave a substantial mark that not only affects the line of putt but also damages the green surface. Spike marks are something that can be avoided if golfers would remember to pick up their feet on the greens.

That said, the penalty for repairing spike marks is two strokes in stroke play, loss of hole in match play.

The Right Move: Obviously, don't tap down spike marks. But I think I need to go beyond just telling you that. This is one of those areas where, in a lot of friendly games, everyone tacitly agrees that it's okay to tap them down. This is bad for a few reasons. First, it's a rules violation. Second, you'll be slowing down play. Third, and maybe most significantly in my opinion, you'll be hurting yourself whenever you play in any official match, whether it's in your club championship, or a member-guest, or any local tournament. If you're in the habit of tapping spike marks, like anything else it's a hard habit to break. You might be doing it without even realizing it, so you run the risk of taking a penalty. In addition to that, it will hurt your confidence on short putts, just knowing that you can't repair those spike marks. You'll feel like you're suddenly at a disadvantage, and chances are you'll putt worse for that reason.

By the way, if you get irked when a putt misses because it hit a spike mark, it will help you to realize something. Spike marks don't only keep good putts from staying out, they can also help guide a slightly off-line putt into the hole. It happens all the time. Nobody ever admits it, though. So maybe in the long run spike marks really aren't that big a deal.

A Final Right Move: Remember that after you've holed out, you can repair spike marks. Feel free to do so if you're not holding up play. I know, this doesn't do you any immediate good, since you've already putted out. But at least you'll be helping others, and maybe the idea will get around not to leave spike marks in the first place.

Violation #17: *Changing Golf Ball Brands for Different Holes.* Although this one might be a little less common than in years past, I still see it a lot with amateurs. The player decides to be cagey and switch golf balls depending on the ball's characteristics in relation to the hole coming up. (Or sometimes they just do it to avoid the possibility of hitting a good ball into a water hazard.)

Say, for example, the player is on the tee of a relatively long par three. There's a fifteen-mile-per-hour wind at the player's back, and the pin is tucked on the front of the green, behind a bunker. Ordinarily the player might be thinking of hitting a five-wood here, but with the wind helping, it's a three- or four-iron shot.

So the player is faced with a longish iron shot that must be stopped quickly, downwind, if he wants to keep the ball anywhere in the vicinity of the hole. Accordingly, he takes out the old standard, a wound ball with a soft Balata cover. This ball does the best job of gripping the clubface at impact so that it carries more backspin and lands more softly on the green.

On the next hole, the player turns around to play a long par four that's into that fifteen-mile-per-hour wind. The player knows it takes two strong shots to get home, even with no wind. To make it today he or she will need two perfect hits that are low and running. So he or she puts away the Balata and brings out a "rock"—that is, a two-piece, very hard, Surlyn-covered ball. This type of ball shoots off the clubface with very little backspin. It does the best job of boring through a stiff headwind, staying low, and giving extra yards in roll. Therefore it gives the player at least a chance to reach the green in two shots.

All of the above strategy makes good sense. There's only one problem. Most people think it's illegal. You deserve some good news right about now and you're going to get it. Unless the one-ball rule is specifically stated at your club, there is no penalty for changing brands.

Violation #18: *"Rolling Starts" While Another Player Is Hitting.* This is a breach of etiquette, not a rule that carries any specific penalty. But I know it's one that ticks off a lot of players, especially on Tour. It can happen anywhere on the course but is most likely to happen at the tee, where all members of the group are close together.

What happens is that a player who has already hit his or her tee shot starts walking just a fraction of a second before the last player to hit has completed his or her shot. It's almost an infinitesimal thing. The player who's standing maybe two yards away from the player making the shot starts to take a step toward the fairway in sync with the start of the player's downswing.

Now, a defense can be made that, if the player has started his or her downswing, nothing anybody else does can affect the shot. So you might say, what's the big deal? To the player who's hitting the shot and notices that step it could be a very big deal, particularly if they've flubbed the shot. He or she will undoubtedly believe that the player who moved caused them to miss the shot, and bad blood often ensues.

The Penalty: There's no penalty under the rules for this breach of etiquette. But it's a move that, for anyone who does it habitually, is not going to win them any friends on the golf course. They may actually get "penalized" later on, by a loud cough at the top of their own backswing, or assorted other "head game" retaliations that really cheapen the game, in my opinion.

The Right Move: Whenever you've played your shot and are waiting for somebody else, don't move until they've completed their swing. Those "rolling starts" may not actually hurt a player's shot (and sure, the player might exaggerate as to when he or she saw you move and how much effect it had). But when you start walking while someone else is still swinging, you're showing a basic lack of respect for that other player. It's as if you're saying, "I really can't be bothered with your part in this game. Me and my golf ball are the only things that matter." So if you have been rolling off the tee early, all I can say is, knock it off. And for once in your life, act like a "white-collar" gentleman.

Violation #19: *Sloppy Flag Tending.* This is another etiquette no-no rather than a rules breach. Player A is the first to putt. He or she is lining up a long putt and wants the flag attended so he or she can see the target better. Player B shuffles up to the cup (probably leaving spike marks) and stands anywhere while grabbing the flagstick with one hand. There are three things Player B might have done that can bother the other members of the foursome. One, Player B didn't look where he or she was walking in going to the cup. Chances are good he or she walked on at least one player's line. Two, Player B is not paying attention to where he or she is standing in relation to anyone's line while attending the flag. There's a good chance Player B is standing in someone's line. Three, Player B might be standing to the side of the hole where his or her shadow falls over the hole. This makes it hard for Player A, the putter, to see the cup.

The Penalty: There is no penalty for any of these breaches, except maybe for a few dirty looks from other members of your group. They also know you don't know how to tend a flag.

The Right Move: When someone asks you to attend the flag, be alert to the following points before doing so. First, be aware of where each player's ball (including your own!) is situated on the green. Walk around these lines of putt rather than across any of them. It's best if you approach the hole from a side nobody's putting from. Second, as you approach the cup area to hold the flag, make sure not to plant yourself in anyone's line (again, including your own). By approaching the flag from the "back" side, you can stand a little ways behind the flag and reach forward to hold it, while assuring you haven't stepped in somebody's line. Third, if it's a sunny day, notice where your shadow is falling. If it falls over the cup, step behind the hole and move to the other side of the flag. This will put your shadow away from the hole so Player A can get a good look at the target—which is why you're holding the flag in the first place.

Of course, don't forget to pull the pin out before the ball gets there. If Player A's putt from on the green hits the flagstick, he or she incurs a two-shot penalty or loss of hole in match play. You won't win many friends by not taking the pin out.

Violation #20: *Noisemakers.* You've heard them as you're about to play your shot—jingling change in an opponent's pocket, the ripping sound of someone tearing off the Velcro fastener of their glove, somebody dropping their golf bag to the ground. These noises made by others cause many golfers to do a slow burn. Not only because of the noise itself, but because they may have been purposely timed to upset you.

Sometimes these "noisemakers" are unwitting errors. There are certain players who are nervous by nature, who may jingle coins without realizing they're doing it. This can be true of members of your foursome. So, first, just a reminder to all of you: Be aware of any innocent nervous habits that might interfere with the play of others in your group.

However, I'll add that more often "noisemakers" are conscious movements designed to rattle opponents. You might think I have a very lighthearted approach to golf, and in a lot of ways I do. But there's no way I support the "gamesmanship" seen in many "friendly" matches, which include actions deliberately aimed at throwing off the opponent. Stay above that type of thing. Golf is too fine a game for this garbage. Take pride in playing well and winning matches with your skill, not with tacky tricks.

RULES TO ABIDE BY ON THAT RARE OCCASION WHEN YOU'RE A GUEST AT YOUR WHITE-COLLAR EMPLOYER'S STUFFY PRIVATE CLUB

On the Course

Rule One: When you're ready to crack open that first beer of the day on the second tee or so, make sure not to open the can during the boss's backswing. He'll remember that popping sound for a long time.

Rule Two: Be careful when you step on the gas pedal of your golf cart. Sometimes they take off much faster than you think. You don't want your beer splashing all over your boss's expensive Ralph Lauren golf shirt.

Rule Three: Always start braking the cart a little before you reach your ball. This way there's no chance of a sudden stop, with your half-smoked cheap stogie popping out of your mouth and burning a hole in the boss's $500 knickers.

Aside from those minor limitations (along with some reasonable limits on cursing and club throwing), go ahead and have a great time on the links.

At the Nineteenth Hole

Rule One: Don't ever tell any of the following over-familiar jokes in the company of your boss and/or his clients.

1. "How was your round, honey?" a wife asked her husband after he'd returned from his regular Sunday morning game.

"It was terrible," he answered. "There we were on the third tee when all of a sudden Frank keels over dead of a heart attack!"

"Oh, my, that is terrible!"

"It sure was—for the next sixteen holes it was hit the ball, drag Frank; hit the ball, drag Frank."

2. Why did the golfer wear two pairs of pants?
In case he got a hole in one.

3. An elderly gent of seventy-five was dejected over the fact that his failing eyesight no longer let him see where his ball was going. "I'll tell you what, Mr. Jones," said the club pro. "I'll fix you up with Mr. Riley. He's ninety-five, but still has great eyesight and loves the game." So the two men headed for the first tee. Hitting first, Jones cracked what felt like a good one. "Did you see it, did you see it?" he asked excitedly. "Yeah, I saw it," said the older man slowly. "Then where did it go?" asked his partner. "I don't remember," he answered.

I AM THE WALRUS

4. A foursome of men had been playing golf every Saturday morning for years. One day, as they were putting out on the fourteenth hole, a funeral procession made its way slowly by on a road that ran right past the green. One of the men, addressing his putt, suddenly laid his putter down, took off his hat, and stood quietly with his head bowed until the hearse was out of sight. Then he picked up his club and stroked his ball into the cup. On the next tee, one of his playing partners put a hand on his shoulder and said, "Joe, I have to tell you that was a very touching show of respect you paid on the last green." The other two agreed. "Well, it was the least I could do, fellows," he answered. "After all, I was married to the woman for forty-two years."

5. A husband and wife were playing golf together one day when they reached the tee of the fourth hole, a par four. Reaching back to hit a big drive, the husband sliced his ball well right. When he got to it, he found that a large barn was blocking his shot to the green. "Honey," he said to his wife. "Do me a favor and go over to that barn and open the front doors and open the back doors. Then I'll be able to hit my ball right through it and onto the green." Having done so, his wife stepped back while her husband addressed the ball. He swung, but pulled the shot slightly. It hit the barn and ricocheted off, hitting his wife in the head and killing her instantly.

A few weeks later he was out on the course again, this time with his boss and an associate. When they reached the fourth hole, his boss sliced his drive right behind the barn. Surveying the situation, the boss looked at the associate and said, "Say, would you mind going over to that barn and opening the front doors and then the back doors? Then I'll be able to hit my shot right through it to the green." At this, his junior executive, remembering his own shot from two weeks before, blurted out in a pleading voice, "Boss, please don't try it. I attempted the same thing from this very spot two weeks ago—and I made double bogey."

6. A few deer were grazing in the rough on the second hole of a course known for its poor players. As a group advanced toward the tee, one deer said to the others, "We'd better move out of the way or we may get hit."

"Right," responded another. "Let's all get into the middle of the fairway—we should be safe enough there!"

7. One day a beginning golfer was out on the course by himself, spraying balls everywhere, when he met up with another player who was a low-handicapper. After a couple of holes the good player could see that his new partner wasn't enjoying himself, mainly because his errant shots were costing him an average of one lost ball per hole. "This is even worse than usual," the hacker said with a moan. "If we don't finish soon, I'm going to run out of balls first."

"I'll tell you what I'm going to do for you," said his new friend. "I have a ball here that's just what you need. Say you knock it into the woods. It's got a little pair of legs that pop out and carry it back to the edge of the fairway. Say you hit it into a pond. Then a little pair of flippers appear that propel it to the edge of the water, where the legs walk it back up onto shore. I'm going to give this ball to you, since I hit pretty straight and don't really need it."

"No kidding? This ball will do all that?"

"I've seen it myself."

"Where did you get it?"

"Oh, I found it."

Rule Two: If your boss happens to tell you any of these jokes, just laugh hysterically along with him.

Rule Three: Don't just order a beer. Impress your boss by ordering a Seventeenth Green. This drink was created in honor of the notorious par-three seventeenth hole at the Tournament Players' Club in Ponte Vedra, Florida.

> Impress the bartender by telling him how to make it:
> *3/4 oz. Midori*
> *1/2 oz. vodka*
> *1/2 oz. Triple Sec*
> *1/2 oz. Southern Comfort*
> *cranberry juice*

Fill a twelve-ounce stem glass with ice. Pour liquors in in the above order, but do not stir! Gently fill to top with cranberry juice. Midori should remain separate at the bottom. Garnish with a slice of honeydew melon and a strawberry.

5 SUPERTIPS:

Quick Tips on Shotmaking Techniques for the Golfer on the Run

In Chapter Two I discussed the things you can do to overcome the drudgery of practice and make your sessions as productive as possible. In this chapter I'll show you how to execute the many different types of shots you'll encounter in the course of your rounds.

Now, I think I've made it clear that I have a mind-set pretty similar to that of the average, everyday blue-collar player. I've never been one to dissect the golf swing as if it were an advanced lesson in physics. I'm convinced that a high percentage of golfers never reach their potential because they over-analyze the golf swing. It doesn't take long for you to lose your rhythm and swing flow if you're thinking of count-less positions you need to get into at one point or another during the swing.

Instead, let's be realistic about your swing, just as we've been realistic about how much time you're likely to have to practice. My intent isn't to help you build a gorgeous golf swing like Tom Purtzer's. Heck, I can't even do that for myself! Instead, what I want to give you are some simple, easy-to-understand supertips that will help you play those standard everyday shots better and more easily out on the course.

My supertips will fall into four major shotmaking areas.

- Driving
- Iron Play
- Short Game
- Putting

These tips will prove very useful to you, since you don't have the hours you'd like to devote toward perfecting your swing. As a bonus, each shotmaking area includes at least a couple of *superquick tips*— for those of you who like your instruction in small doses.

DRIVING
Supertip #1: Drive the Nail

A key to good driving is to contact the ball with the driver clubhead traveling on a path virtually level with the ground. This means the club will impart the greatest amount of forward momentum to the ball with the least amount of backspin, which is what you want.

A good mental image is to think of your driver as a hammerhead. Imagine you want to drive a nail squarely into the back of the ball. This image will help you smooth out any tendency to chop downward on the ball and cost you distance.

Supertip #2: Hit the Draw on Dogleg Lefts

Being able to draw the ball when the hole doglegs left not only helps you keep the ball in play but trims yardage from the hole, so you can hit a shorter club for your approach.

To draw the shot, your body alignment should be parallel to a line drawn down the center of the fairway. This is the line you want the shot to start on. Next, align the leading edge of your clubface so it points to the spot where you want the ball to finish, around the dogleg. This means it will be closed in relation to your body alignment. The more you want the shot to draw, the more you close the clubface in relation to your alignment.

Having made this adjustment, swing normally. With good contact, the ball will start down the middle, then start curving left as it peaks and starts its descent.

If you trust this adjustment in clubface alignment as well as the swing itself, you'll be pleasantly surprised with the results.

Supertip #3: Fade the Ball the Easy Way

When a hole doglegs right and a straight shot might put you through the fairway, a controlled fade will keep the ball in the short grass as well as shorten the hole.

Align your body exactly as you would for the draw, straight down the center line. Instead of closing the clubface, open it at address so it's pointing right where you want the ball to finish, around that right-hand curve. The more open the clubface in relation to your body alignment, the more the ball will fade.

Again, the swing itself stays the same. Just try to hit the shot solidly. Trust the slight left-to-right sidespin imparted by the open clubface alignment to give you the curve you're looking for.

Supertip #4: Play the Ball Forward When Driving Downwind

When the wind's at your back off the tee, you've got to take advantage of it. To get a big yardage boost, all you need is to get the ball up in the air a little quicker than normal—get some "air under it," so to speak.

You really don't need to change your swing at all to take advantage of the wind. Instead, play the ball a bit more forward in your driver stance than usual. If, like me, you normally play the ball just behind your left heel, move it forward so it's just ahead of a line drawn to the left heel. This will help you make contact just after your clubhead has reached its lowest point and is starting upward. You'll launch the ball at a higher angle so the wind helps it right away.

Last, when you move the ball up in your stance, tee it just a fraction of an inch higher than normal.

Supertip #5: How to Square the Clubface at Impact

Many weekend players lose distance and accuracy because they never get the clubface back to square at impact. When the clubface is left open, the con-

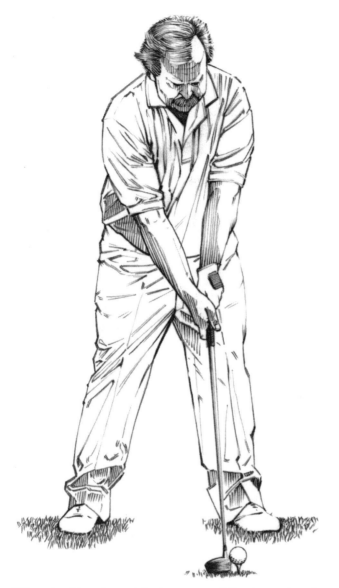

When looking for added power off the tee, play the ball forward in your stance.

tact is not as flush and the ball is either pushed or push-sliced weakly to the right.

This fault is often caused by the player lunging toward the target on the downswing, usually because he or she is trying to hit the ball hard. This puts the body ahead of its original address position, so the clubhead is forced into an exaggerated open position at impact.

To correct this flaw, rotate the left hip around and to the left on the downswing, rather than driving it at the target. This hip rotation creates room for your arms and hands to swing freely through the impact zone. As a result, the clubface works from open before impact, to square at impact, and back to closed after the ball has been struck. Straighter shots result.

☞ **SUPERQUICK TIP:** *When setting up to drive, your left arm and the clubshaft should virtually form a straight line down to the ball, and your head should be completely behind the ball.*

Supertip #6: Pick the Right Driver Loft

Many weekenders make their tee shots harder than they should be by swinging a driver with too little loft. Subconsciously, they know this is the case, and they try to scoop or lift the ball instead of swinging right through it.

The more clubhead speed you generate and the farther you can carry the ball, the less loft you'll need. Following are the driver loft ranges you should use depending on your normal carry on tee shots.

I AM THE WALRUS

Average Carry	Loft Range
150 yards	15–16 degrees
175 yards	13–14 degrees
200 yards	11–12 degrees
225 yards and up	8–10 degrees

Most of the metalwoods manufactured today indicate the club's loft angle. Make sure you pick one that allows you to comfortably hit the ball into the air.

Supertip #7: Aim Away from Trouble

You may have heard pros advise that you should aim toward the trouble, then curve the ball away from it. I disagree, especially for the weekend player. There's too much risk and too high a skill level required. What if you hit the ball dead straight and it doesn't curve the way you planned?

If the extreme trouble is on the left side, tee your ball on the left side of the teeing area. Aim away from trouble, toward the right side of the fairway, and just try to hit a solid straight shot. If you hook it a little you'll be fine, and if you fade it, you're only in the rough and will still have a shot. When trouble lurks on the right, do the opposite: Tee the ball on the right side of the tee, then hit straight for the left side of the fairway.

Supertip #8: Swing to a Full Finish

All good drivers swing the club freely *through* the ball rather than at it. If you're hitting at the ball, you're actually decelerating the club at impact. This means not only a loss of power, but loss of accuracy as well.

Craig Stadler

Good driving skills demand that you swing into a full finish.

Instead of being mesmerized by the ball at address, focus on swinging into a full finish. Then swing the clubhead right through the ball. At the finish you should be in perfect balance. Nearly all your weight should be on your left foot, you should be up on your right toe, and your entire body should face the target with the clubshaft hanging down behind you.

Remember to swing through to this full finish po-

I AM THE WALRUS

sition and you'll get the most out of your swing through impact, where it counts.

☞ **SUPERQUICK TIP:** *On holes with hilly landing areas, use the club (not necessarily the driver) that will leave you with a level lie for your second shot.*

IRON PLAY

Supertip #9: Punch It from Tight Lies

For the public course player who regularly encounters less than perfect playing conditions, the ability to play shots off thin grass or off hardpan is a big plus.

This shot isn't as hard as many golfers make it. Handicap players often try to pick the ball cleanly off a bare lie, but the more reliable method is to play the *punch* shot.

Again, the adjustment you make in your address position will help define the correct swing motion for this shot. Use the same length club as from a normal lie and move the ball back in your stance two or three inches. Your hands will be more ahead of the ball than normal at address. From this position your takeaway, backswing, and downswing will automatically be steeper than normal. The clubface will trap the ball against the ground at impact so that the shot takes off in a low trajectory, but with lots of backspin and control.

Supertip #10: Play Smart to Tightly Guarded Flags

Always take the shot situation as well as your own shotmaking strengths and skill level into account before deciding when to attack a tough pin position.

When hitting off hardpan, play the ball back in your
stance, with your hands well ahead of it.

First, consider your skill level. If you're a high-handicapper and don't have a lot of confidence in your iron play, don't challenge a tough pin. Your best bet is to try to land the ball on the middle of the green every time.

If you're a low-handicapper, you obviously have more options to consider. For a short iron shot, you may be able to hit the ball high and soft enough that it's reasonable to go for the pin. But if it's a long iron shot, again the smart play may be to shade toward the middle of the green.

Another factor is where the pin is positioned. If it's tucked left and you draw the ball with confidence, you can play an attacking shot. If you fade your irons, play for the fat part.

Finally, always go with your instincts. If you have doubts about going for a tightly tucked pin, those doubts will probably be reflected in your swing. Plan a shot that you're one hundred percent confident you can hit.

Supertip #11: Shorten Your Swing on Iron Shots

I never hit an iron shot from the fairway as hard as I can. Neither should you. You'll get the ball consistently closer to the hole if you learn to make a three-quarter swing on all normal iron shots.

Whatever the length of your full swing, make up your mind to go only three quarters of that distance back with your irons. This will keep you centered over the ball with less weight shift on both the backswing and downswing. After impact you should finish in a nicely balanced position on your left foot. The clubshaft will be in front of you rather than

To hit solid, supercontrolled iron shots, employ a three-quarter swing.

over your shoulder because of the lesser momentum through the impact zone.

You'll hit the ball much more solidly—and hit many more greens—by keeping your iron swing at the three-quarter mark.

☞ **SUPERQUICK TIP:** *From fairway bunkers, concentrate on the front of the ball rather than the back of it. This will help you swing the club down the target line and sweep the ball cleanly off the sand.*

Supertip #12: Sweep, Don't Weep

Most players' woes with the long irons stem from a faulty address position. Unless you're strong as an ox, you can't hit down successfully with these clubs and expect to get them nicely airborne. You need to catch these shots right at the bottom of the swing so that the full loft of the club is utilized.

At address, play the ball opposite the lowest point in your swing, usually opposite the inside of the left heel. Position your hands even with the clubface rather than ahead of it, so you don't reduce the club's effective loft. Then make a smooth swing and just try to clip the ball off the grass, as if you were hitting off an expensive carpet. An improved flight with the long irons will result.

Supertip #13: Hit Down on Divot Shots

It's inevitable that you will, one day, find your ball in a "divot hole" on the fairway. When you do, once you finish cursing a blue streak, get the most out of the shot by doing the following.

Craig Stadler

1. Judge what club you'd normally need to reach the green.

2. Select one club shorter than you'd take from a good lie (for example, a six-iron instead of a five).

3. Address the ball with your weight more on your forward foot than normal, and position the ball just behind the center point of your stance. (This reduces the club's loft, effectively turning a six-iron into a five.)

4. As with the punched iron shot, make an upright swing and strike down on the ball sharply.

☞ **SUPERQUICK TIP:** *When the greens get hard in mid-to-late summer, take one club less and play a punch shot whenever you have an opening at the front of the green.*

Supertip #14: Keep the Swing Upright

With the shorter irons your primary goal is accuracy. That's why I recommend that you develop a more upright swinging action with these clubs.

I swing my arms and the club on an upright plane even though I'm not particularly tall. Why? Basically, the more upright the swing plane, the longer the clubhead will travel along the target line through the impact zone. Thus, the greater arm swing allows you to hit down on the ball rather than sweep it. This is an advantage when playing from very deep rough and also from down lies in the fairway.

As you turn away from the ball, consciously swing your arms toward the sky, more upward than around the body. Coming down, pull the club down and through the ball with the back of your left hand leading the clubface. You'll find more shots taking off straight for the flag.

Supertip #15: Make Club Selection a Priority

You probably know that if you're hitting a shot uphill you need to take "more club," while if the shot's downhill, you need "less club." But here's a little-known fact to help you fine-tune your hilly-course club selection.

For long iron or wood shots that are steeply uphill or downhill, take two clubs more or less, respectively. Why? Because with the longer clubs the ball will be coming down on a much flatter trajectory. So, downhill, its parabola has room to shoot forward a lot farther. Uphill, that longer parabola is cut off more quickly.

Use this knowledge when playing hilly courses and you'll have the edge on your competition.

☞ **SUPERQUICK TIP:** *When you need to increase your clubhead speed and hit an iron farther than normal, grip the club more lightly.*

Supertip #16: Always Tee Up the Ball on Par-Three Holes

Whenever you're hitting from the tee of a par three, tee up the ball.

You'll often see amateur golfers drop the ball onto the teeing area and play it from there. There's no advantage to this. Any time you can use a tee, do so, because it ensures you'll make clean contact without any grass getting caught between clubface and ball.

Craig Stadler

Teeing the ball also helps because you can hit a higher, softer-landing shot, and thus play more aggressively at the flag.

On short iron shots, tee the ball just above the grass or one-quarter inch in height.

For long iron tee shots, tee the ball about a half-inch high.

For a low, driving shot, tip the tee slightly forward.

For a high, soft shot, downwind or to a tight pin placement, tip the tee slightly back.

SHORT GAME

Supertip #17: Hole It!

For the basic, short greenside chip, don't adopt the attitude that you're just trying to get the ball up and down. Instead, try to hole it!

The short chip is just like a medium-to-long putt. You're simply lofting the ball over the fringe, and from there it runs like a putt toward the cup. You should try just as hard to hole this shot as you would a putt of the same length. First, read the chip just like you would a putt. Then align the leading edge of your chipping club as accurately as possible to the starting line you've determined.

Finally, to give yourself the best possible chance to hole out, check the pin to see how it's lying. If it's resting toward you, take it out, since this might keep your perfect chip from going in.

Supertip #18: Make the Sand Do the Work

The greenside sand shot from a normal lie is about the easiest shot in golf. Maybe amateurs have

An image of the sand lifting the ball high into the air will help you employ the correct bunker technique.

so much trouble hitting it because they don't understand what a blast from sand really entails.

Basically, all you want to do is slap the sand with the club about two inches behind the ball. Imagine spraying a shower of sand out of the trap, and picture the ball as just an extrabig grain of the sand that gets showered out.

Once you become confident with this basic image and with your sand-slapping action, you'll quickly learn to play long and short sand shots, simply by slapping the sand with a fuller or shorter swing.

Supertip #19: Stop It!

When you face a longish greenside pitch from rough over a bunker, you'll need a high-lofted shot to stop the ball near the pin.

First, make sure your lie is fairly good, with a little cushion so you can get the leading edge of your wedge underneath the ball. Next, open your stance and the blade of your wedge. The higher and softer the shot you need, the more open both should be.

Play the shot almost like the bunker shot, slapping the wedge into the grass just behind the ball. Impact will inevitably be muffled somewhat, so strive for a full follow-through to encourage ample clubhead acceleration. The ball will come out high and drop softly, so you should be able to hit the ball close no matter where the pin is located.

Supertip #20: Play the Down-Lie Dig

Sometimes you'll find yourself in the same position as described above, except that the ball is snuggled deep in the rough. It's important to realize that

Strive for a full follow-through when playing the "stop" shot.

in this case you shouldn't go with the open-faced flip. There's too much risk of blading the ball over the green from this lie.

Instead, align yourself more squarely to your target with the ball about in the middle of your stance. Set the blade of your wedge square to the flag with your hands slightly ahead of the ball. (*Note:* If you have an L-wedge, this is a good time to use it because it has more loft than a sand wedge, and also a smaller flange so it's less likely to bounce at impact.) Your left hand should control the shot, pushing the club back in an upright arc and pulling the clubhead down and through the ball. Make sure to keep a firm grip with the last three fingers of that hand, as well as a steady head.

The ball will come out on a slightly lower trajectory and will run more than the flip shot. If the pin is tucked close over the bunker, be content to let the shot run a little past the hole, rather than trying to get cute and risk hitting into sand. You'll save strokes in the long run.

☞ **SUPERQUICK TIP:** *When chipping with the sand wedge, always hood the clubface slightly. This keeps the protruding back edge of the flange from scuffing the ground before impact.*

Supertip #21: Run the Ball

When your ball is on the fringe with the pin a long distance away, play a running rather than a lofted chip. Your aim is to carry the ball a short distance onto the green and let it run to the hole. So follow these simple steps.

1. Pick the iron you like to run the ball with.

2. Visualize a spot you need to land the ball on that will allow it to run the correct distance to the cup.

3. Try to land the ball right at that spot.

A couple of fine points for this shot:

- Check the lie. If it's fluffy, the ball will run a little farther than normal.

- Avoid landing the ball on a severe slope. This makes it difficult to judge how far it will roll. Play a more or less lofted chip if it allows you to land the ball on a flat spot, making it easier to control the total distance of the shot.

Supertip #22: Play the Skip-Wedge Pitch

Occasionally you'll face a pitch to a pin on the top tier of a firm, fast-running green. You can't loft the ball to the top tier and expect it to stop. The best way to hit the ball close to the hole is with a lower pitch that skips up to the top tier, then brakes to a halt.

Play the skip-wedge pitch with a pitching wedge. As with the iron shot from hardpan discussed earlier, move the ball back of center in your stance and keep the hands ahead at address.

Swing the club back mainly with your arms while keeping your head steady.

Swing the club down into the back of the ball. Keep the follow-through low with the club pointing to the target.

When executed properly, the ball will dart out on a low trajectory, so you might even think it's going too far. However, it will carry plenty of backspin

A steady head is critical to playing the "skip" shot.

and pull up to a quick stop after taking one big bounce.

Supertip #23: Take It to the Bank

On courses with raised greens, you might face a recovery shot complicated by a bank between you and the green. You can pitch the ball over the bank, but it may be impossible to stop it close to the hole. If this is the case, play the bank shot. My tips on executing this shot are as follows:

- Play the ball back in your stance with your hands ahead of it, so you make crisp contact, catching the ball first.

- Judge the bank carefully. If it's steep, use less loft (a five- or six-iron). Chip the ball firmly, landing it lower down on the bank so it can run more.Conversely, if the grade's not too steep, you can use a bit more loft (seven- or eight-iron) and carry the ball farther up the bank.

- Study the depth of the grass on the bank to help judge how hard to hit the ball.

- If you must err, err on the side of hitting too firmly, so the ball doesn't roll back to your feet.

☞ **SUPERQUICK TIP:** *From uphill or downhill lies in bunkers, always position the ball in your stance more toward your higher foot.*

Supertip #24: Belly It

A shot that causes many amateurs grief occurs when the ball comes to rest on the fringe, right up against the first cut of rough. Either a putt or a standard chip fails because the club gets caught in the grass behind the ball.

Craig Stadler

It's simple to get out of this course predicament if you "belly" the ball—strike it at its equator with the leading edge of your sand wedge.

Address the ball with the leading edge of your wedge behind the ball's equator, just above the rough. Keeping your head steady, hit the ball with the leading edge, using the same force of stroke you'd use with the putter. The club contacts the ball only and the ball rolls very smoothly.

PUTTING

Supertip #25: Forefinger Feel

The putting grip is one of the most individualized areas of golf technique—there are limitless styles. I've always used and highly recommend the hold that's sometimes referred to as the "Old Man's Grip" or the "Over-Forty Grip."

The distinguishing feature is the position of the right forefinger. Instead of wrapping it around the handle as in the normal overlapping grip for full shots, place the forefinger down the rear of the shaft. This finger acts like a pointer or a guide, helping you push the putter's clubface directly toward your target.

Try some practice putts with the right forefinger along the back of the grip. You'll immediately sense how it guides and supports the stroke and allows you to putt with confidence.

Supertip #26: Halve the Speed

On putts of forty feet and longer, getting the right feel of how hard to stroke the ball can be difficult. Here's a tip that will help.

This old man's finger-grip will help you guide the putter along the correct line.

After inspecting the line of, say, a forty-foot putt, walk from the ball to a point twenty feet along the target line. Take a practice stroke with what you think is the right amount of force needed to putt the ball to the hole from that spot. Then walk back to where your ball is resting. Add the force of the stroke for the remaining twenty feet of the putt to the stroke force you calculated for the "second" twenty feet. Since you can pretty confidently esti-mate the stroke force needed from twenty feet, you'll have a lot more confidence by adding the force for the two "halves" of the putt, rather than guessing at one long distance.

☞ **SUPERQUICK TIP:** *When you miss a long putt, carefully watch what the ball does as it rolls past the hole. This will help you read the break and sink your next putt.*

Supertip #27: Putt Like a Pendulum

The most reliable putting stroke is one that moves like a pendulum on a grandfather clock. Whatever the length of putt and amount of force required, the backstroke and downstroke should be exactly the same length. The reason is that you'll be assured of maintaining an even tempo.

If you take too short a backstroke, you'll instinctively shove the putter through the impact zone and almost always hit the ball off line. When you employ a longer backstroke than you need, you'll decelerate the putter coming into impact, and leave the ball short of the hole.

A good drill to help develop the perfect pendulum stroke is to set a yardstick down on a practice green along a line to the hole. Then measure to make sure no matter what the putt's length, your backstroke and downstroke are the same number of inches in length.

Supertip #28: Stroke It Up

When you hit a ball on the upstroke, it begins rolling with overspin immediately. This gives the putt a smooth start and the best chance to hold its line.

To promote this type of hit, simply move the ball

forward in your stance—approximately at a point opposite your left heel, or instep, if that works better.

Supertip #29: Manage the Speed of Your Putts

Three-putt greens are caused much more frequently by an error in the speed of the roll rather than being way off line with the putt. Therefore, practice time spent on controlling speed is obviously very valuable. Here's a speed-control game to play during your practice sessions. Take one ball to the practice putting green. Let's say the green has nine holes. Putt to each of them in succession. Your goal (besides making the putt) is to hit each putt so that it reaches the hole, but does not go by the hole by more than three feet.

If you learn to ingrain this speed into all the putts you face, you'll improve your putting in two ways.

1. You won't three-putt often because any second putts will be three feet or less.

2. You'll actually sink a lot more putts because all your putts will have reached the hole, and therefore have a chance to go in, and no putts will be rolling so fast that they will jump out of the hole if they are right on line.

☞ **SUPERQUICK TIP:** *On putts of three feet or less, always make a stroke that's firm enough so that the ball hits the back of the hole.*

Supertip #30: Play It Straight When It's Wet

Whenever you're putting on wet greens, either in rain or early-morning dew, you should play your putts to break less than they normally do.

There are two reasons for this. First, the green

will be slow when it's wet, and a slow putt won't break as much as a faster one. Second, when you roll a ball over a wet surface, the center of the ball—the part rolling end-over-end—picks up moisture and weight. This gives the ball a sort of gyroscope effect. The ball will tend to keep rolling end-over-end and will be affected even less than usual by any contours in the green.

For short putts on wet greens, make especially sure to stroke firmly and play for only a limited amount of break.

Supertip #31: Toe It

Solid impact between the putter's face and the ball is vital to rolling the ball on the intended line at the correct speed. Yet few people work on improving this.

Here's a practice technique to help you hit your putts solidly. Stroke the ball with the toe of the putter, rather than the clubface itself. This drill forces you to contact the back of the ball with a very small hitting area. If you don't hit the ball dead center, you'll know it immediately because the ball will veer off the intended line.

Try to improve your contact until you can hit ten solid putts in a row using the toe of the putter. If you can accomplish this, when you return to the course and revert to your normal style, you'll see improvements in your concentration, stroking action, and putting scores.

Supertip #32: Watch the Spot

The best way to keep your head steady and improve your putting is to continue watching the spot where the ball was resting before contact.

172

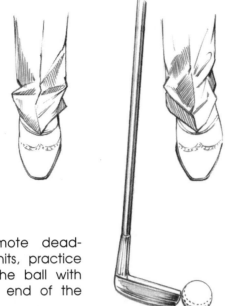

To promote dead-center hits, practice hitting the ball with the toe end of the putter.

This type of discipline may not seem necessary, but it is. Almost every high-handicap golfer tends to peek at their putts a little earlier than they think they do. Holding your head steady for that one extra second is crucial. So watch the spot until well after the stroke is completed, and listen for the sound of more putts dropping.

A Final Tip: The Fun Fling

Throwing clubs the conventional way is not a good gambit even for the blue-collar player. Studies have shown that this all-out club fling is the cause of twenty percent of all accidents that occur on the golf course. You could be suspended from your club for endangering other players. Also, the all-out fling

Letting off steam is one thing. Doing it with class is another.

is dangerous because you could throw out your shoulder and mess up your swing for several weeks or more.

Instead, consider adding the *Fun Fling* to your shotmaking repertoire. Here's how to execute it.

1. After flubbing your shot, maintain a narrow stance right where you played the shot from.

2. Hold the club almost as if in the address position, except that the clubhead is about one foot off the ground.

3. Use good etiquette. Check to make sure no one else in your foursome is within twenty feet of your target area.

4. Stand silently for a second, gathering explosive energy.

5. Keeping a perfectly still head and with no body movement, give the club a quick jerk upward, using a very wristy stroke and a full release. There should be no extraneous body movement in this motion.

6. The club should fly high and soft, end-over-end, and with plenty of backspin. Practice this shot frequently and you'll soon be putting it within ten feet of your bag every time.

BIOGRAPHIES

JOHN ANDRISANI is the senior editor of instruction at *Golf Magazine* and a former assistant editor of Britain's *Golf Illustrated* magazine.

Andrisani has co-authored major instruction books with the game's top tour pros: *Learning Golf: The Lyle Way* with Sandy Lyle; *Natural Golf* with Seve Ballesteros; *101 Supershots* with Chi Chi Rodriguez; *Grip It and Rip It!* with John Daly; and *Total Shotmaking* with Fred Couples. He is also the co-author of *The Golf Doctor* with Robin McMillan; *Hit It Hard!* with power hitter Mike Dunaway; and *Golf Your Way,* an Encyclopedia of Instruction, with renowned teacher Phil Ritson.

Andrisani's popular instructional articles and humorous golf stories have appeared in golfing and non-golfing publications worldwide, including *Golf France* and *Playboy* magazine.

A former winner of the American Golf Writer's Championship, Andrisani plays off a 6-handicap at Lake Nona Golf Club in Orlando, Florida.

Andrisani was selected to appear in *Who's Who in America* for 1992 and 1993.

KEN LEWIS, one of the world's leading illustrators, is best known for his work in golf.

JEFF BLANTON is a Florida-based photographer whose work has appeared in several major golf books and top golf magazines.

176